I0142122

# *Unsung Heroes*

by John Guzzetta

© 2020 Spiritbuilding Publishers

All rights reserved. No part of this book may be reproduced in any form without written permission of the publishers.

Published by

**Spiritbuilding Publishers**

9700 Ferry Road

Waynesville, Ohio 45068


Printed in the United States of America

UNSUNG HEROES

by John Guzzetta


ISBN 978–0–9990684–1–0

# Spiritbuilding

## PUBLISHERS

Spiritual equipment for the contest of life

# Table of Contents

# Introduction

WE KNOW A LOT ABOUT the major characters of the New Testament: Paul, Peter, James, John, etc., and of course the Lord Jesus Himself. I've attended uplifting and fruitful quarter-long studies of Paul and his journeys, and of the Twelve Apostles.

Also sprinkled among the pages of the New Testament are names mentioned almost in passing, quick references to people whose duties and deeds are not given much attention, people like Onesimus, Tertius, Phoebe. We tend to overlook them, but the Holy Spirit includes them for a reason. With a little study and thought, we discover they were involved in vital areas of spiritual work.

This book is an effort to present thoughts on the "minor" characters of Acts and the Epistles. If the Holy Spirit includes these names for our benefit, what lessons can we tease out of them (without going too far) that inform our faith and inspire us to good works?

I have a reason that goes beyond curiosity. Many times, I've heard Christians say, "I can't be an elder, or a preacher, or *that* preacher, so I guess I'll just be happy to sit on this pew." That's the wrong idea!

Sometimes a congregation does not do a very good job encouraging people to explore their talents, nor motivating people to employ those talents. Sometimes a congregation wishes to protect new converts or weak members from being taxed with work. We worry that walking up to a new convert and saying, "Hey, I'm going to sign you up to bring food to the funeral Friday night, OK?" or "I've added your name to the duty list to help pass the trays next month, OK?" might drive them away.

There may be an exception here or there, but for most people, being asked to contribute makes that person or family feel like a valuable part of the church. No one likes to sit on the bench for a whole season. The more quickly leaders of a congregation approach new converts to get involved, the more opportunities a congregation provides for them to spread their new wings, the stronger their faith becomes, and the closer they feel to the family of God. In the same verse Lydia was baptized, she began practicing hospitality and contributing to the work of evangelism (Acts 16:15, NASB). In the same town Paul was baptized, he began proclaiming Jesus as the Christ (Acts 9:19–20). People aren't as fragile as we think they are.

There's an old story about a father and young son whose fishing boat flipped over in the waters off New England in January. They managed to get into the small open lifeboat, but were soaked through. They could see the lights of shore several miles away. It would take many hours, but they were confident they could reach shore. The father knocked the ice off the oarlocks, inserted the two oars, and began rowing. After a while, the son said, "Dad, you're beginning to get tired. Let me take a turn at the oars." Dad was feeling guilty for letting the fishing boat capsize, and also wished to spare his son from the backbreaking and repetitive work. So, he instructed his son to curl up in the bow, while he continued to row. Several times over the next few hours, the son offered to take a turn at the oars, and each time the father refused, telling him to relax and be patient, for they would be home soon. The boy grew silent, while the father doggedly rowed on. Several hours later, as dawn was approaching, the father nearly incoherent with fatigue felt the bow of the rowboat touch the shore. With new vigor and excitement he leapt out onto the beach, crying, "We are saved!" But when he attempted to share his joy with his sleeping son, he discovered that he was stiff. He had quietly frozen to death during the night, unnoticed by the father. The father had protected him from the very activity that would have kept him warm and alive.

Everyone needs a turn at the oars.

These character studies convince us that the work of the church—from helping widows to leading worship all the way up to evangelizing of cities—was shared by many, many more people than just Paul and the Apostles. Sometimes the inadequacy is in our own hearts. We look at our place in the church and despair. We see song leaders and preachers with a prominent place on stage. We see elders and deacons with official titles. Is there a spot for anyone else to make a difference? The answer is yes! Every oar is vital.

Even if we can't be Peter or Paul, the alternative is not to sit in a pew, mouth a few songs, drop in a few dollars, and be content until Judgment Day. There is an enormous amount of work to be done. Each and every Christian is placed in the kingdom for a reason. Each and every Christian has an important part to play.

Paul compares the church to a human body:

> Even as the body is one and yet has many members, and all the members of the body, though they are many, are one body, so also is Christ … God has placed the members, each one of them, in the body, just as He desired. If they were all one member, where would the body be? But now there are many members, but one body. And the eye cannot say to the hand, "I have no need of you"; or against the head to the feet, "I have no need of you." On the contrary, it is much truer that the members of the body which seem to be weaker are necessary … Now you are Christ's body, and individually members of it" (1 Corinthians 12:12–27).

You may not happen to be the hands or the tongue—at least not today—but if you are in the body, you are vital to it, whether as an ear or even a foot. My senior year of high school I broke my big toe in the first soccer game; whereas I had never much paid attention to that member of my body before, its inability to support weight and strike a ball now dominated my thoughts for the rest of the season. Every part, no matter how humble it seems, has a part to contribute to the glory of the body of Christ.

Jesus' parable of the talents (Matthew 25:14–30) reminds us that serving the Lord is not about what abilities and blessings we do not possess (2 Corinthians 8:12), but what we do with the talents we do possess. The five-talent man and two-talent man were judged "according to their ability."

The one-talent man was not judged for his apparent lack of ability, but because he didn't use the talent the master gave him. He didn't lose the talent of money, he didn't allow it to be stolen, he didn't squander it, and he didn't gamble it away. He held onto it. But he didn't use what he had to make an increase for his master.

Every Christian has a talent, a "special gift," to use in Christ's service.

> Since we have gifts that differ according to the grace given to us, each of us is to exercise them accordingly: if prophecy, according to the proportion of his faith; if service, in his serving; or he who teaches, in his teaching; or he who exhorts, in his exhortation; he who gives, with liberality; he who leads, with diligence; he who shows mercy, with cheerfulness (Romans 12:6–8).

> As each one has received a special gift, employ it in serving one another as good stewards of the manifold grace of God. Whoever speaks is to do so as one who is speaking the utterances of God; whoever serves is to do so as one who is serving by the strength which God supplies; so that in all things God may be glorified through Jesus Christ, to whom belongs the glory and dominion forever and ever. Amen (1 Peter 4:10–11).

And every part is vital.

> Speaking the truth in love, we are to grow up in all aspects into Him who is the head, even Christ, from whom the whole body, being fitted and held together by what every joint supplies, according to the proper working of each individual part, causes the growth of the body for the building up of itself in love (Ephesians 4:15–16).

This study is an effort to learn what "every joint supplies," to recognize, and celebrate, and emulate the contributions of Christians recorded in Acts and the Epistles that may have escaped our notice before.

Without you, the body of Christ will never become all it could be. Thanks be to God for all those already using their talents in the kingdom. And may we all be encouraged to find ways to do more, and bring others along with us.

## Questions for Thought

1. How does a Christian benefit when he works for the Lord?

2. What happens to a Christian who does not work?

3. What are some key applications of Paul's comparison of the members of the church to the parts of the human body?

4. Does every Christian have a talent, a contribution to make? What do Romans 12:6-8 and 1 Peter 4:10-11 demand?

5. What is one talent that you could better use to the Lord's glory?

# Epaphras:
## *Striving in Prayer*

FROM THE EVIDENCE LUKE PRESENTS in the book of Acts, it seems likely that Paul had never actually visited Colossae, or the two nearby towns of Hierapolis and Laodicea. Paul didn't make it that far west on his first journey, he purposely skirted the area on his second journey (Acts 16:6), and though he was in the vicinity on his third journey (Acts 18:23; 19:1), Luke describes only his work in Ephesus. When Paul writes the letter to Colossae from Roman imprisonment, he mentions "all those who have not personally seen my face" (Colossians 2:1).

If Paul didn't plant the gospel seed in Colossae, who did? Paul's introduction suggests that a Christian named Epaphras had something to do with it.

> We give thanks to God ... since we heard of your faith in Christ Jesus ... which has come to you ... from Epaphras, our beloved fellow bond-servant, who is a faithful servant of Christ on our behalf, and he also informed us of your love in the Spirit (Colossians 1:3–8).

Perhaps Paul sent Epaphras as a missionary, since he was "a faithful servant on our behalf." Later, Paul identifies Epaphras as "one of your number" (4:12). So, I tend to think Epaphras was a resident of the Colossae area who heard the gospel from Paul and then brought it back to his hometown. In any case, Epaphras recently had brought news from Colossae to Paul in Roman custody. Now, he found himself unable to return to the people of Colossae, since he was busy ministering to Paul in his imprisonment. Perhaps, since Paul refers to Epaphras as a "fellow prisoner" (Philemon 23), he shared actual captivity with Paul, whether voluntarily or involuntarily. Paul chose Tychicus and Onesimus instead to bear his letter to Colossae (4:7–9).

Paul wanted the Colossians to know that even though Epaphras was separated from his beloved brethren by distance, he was not separated from them in his heart, nor from his ability to make an impact there. Paul, in his closing comments, reported:

> Epaphras, who is one of your number, a bondslave of Jesus Christ, sends you his greetings, always laboring earnestly for you in his prayers, that you may stand perfect and fully assured in all the will of God. For I testify of him that he has a deep concern for you and for those who are in Laodicea and Hierapolis (Colossians 4:12–13).

Whatever the exact nature of Epaphras' relationship to the Christians in Colossae, Laodicea, and Hierapolis, he didn't let distance prevent him from working. His "deep concern" motivated him to be "always laboring earnestly for you in his prayers."

From time to time, we will receive a request for help from a far-off place. Perhaps a foreign evangelist reports persecutions and threats from the government in his country. Perhaps family members complain of a serious sickness. Perhaps brethren we used to worship with call to talk about troubles in their congregation. Does it seem silly to say, "I can't be there … but I'll be praying for you"?

I hope not! If we understand the purpose and power of prayer, we will understand that prayers are not half-measures. Prayer is the way we communicate with God and the way we get things done; or to say it more accurately, the way we request that God get things done on our behalf. Philippians 4:6 says, "be anxious for nothing, but in everything by prayer and supplication with thanksgiving let your requests be made known to God." Now, it is important to recognize and submit to the will of God when praying (Matthew 26:39; 2 Corinthians 12:8–9; 1 John 5:14; 2 Samuel 12:22). But too often, "you do not have because you do not ask" (James 4:2). Prayer can move God to move mountains for us (Matthew 7:11; 21:21–22; Romans 8:32). Prayer opened Hannah's womb (1 Samuel 1:3–20) and called down fire from heaven (1 Kings 18:36–38). In fact, prayer can even change God's mind (2 Kings 20:1–6; Jeremiah 26:19; Exodus 32:14; Amos 7:1–3)!

Knowing the power of prayer, Epaphras was "laboring earnestly" in prayer. The phrase "laboring earnestly" translates the Greek verb *agonizomai*. Various Greek dictionaries define it "to contend, to strive, straining every nerve to obtain the object" (*Vine's Expository Dictionary of New Testament Words:* Fight, B1), "to put forth great effort to obtain a result" (Renn, *Expository Dictionary of Bible Words*: Strive), "to contend for a prize" (Earle, *Word Meanings in The New Testament*: Col. 4:12). Obviously, our English word "agony" derives from it; and while it's certainly true that some exercise feels like agony, that would be taking the word picture down an unintended direction. The word is used of striving to win athletic contests, such as in 1 Corinthians 9:25, where it is translated "compete." Metaphorically, *agonizomai* suggests putting all the self-discipline and energetic effort of an athlete into a spiritual pursuit, exerting every muscle toward the finish line or final bell. It's the word Paul uses to describe his own efforts to teach the gospel (Colossians 1:29). It's the word Paul uses to spur on Timothy to "fight the good fight" (1 Timothy 6:12).

We often take a lackadaisical approach to prayer. Epaphras was not just off-handedly mentioning the Colossians at mealtimes. He didn't just say, "Lord, be with the Colossians." Instead, we might imagine Epaphras diligently and frequently praying for the Colossians, daily without fail, not for a minute but for a solid hour, with specific concerns in his mind and specific names on his lips. Not just for the usual healing of the sick, but for maturity and assurance, as Paul says, "that you may stand perfect and fully assured in all the will of God." That's a big goal and includes praying for things like greater faith through teaching, for greater love through service, for greater numbers through evangelism, for steadfastness in persecution, for peace and harmony in the family of God. We might imagine Epaphras following a written prayer plan, with all the fortitude of a dieter keeping track of his meals, or an athlete logging miles in preparation for a race.

Brothers and sisters who are looking for something to do: strive in prayer! You can be hundreds of miles away, but Jesus proved that one doesn't need to be standing at the bedside of a sick person to pray for him (Luke 7:2–10). You can be a new Christian and pray effectively, for Paul requested prayers from those he recently ministered to (Romans 15:30). You can be handicapped, without access to a car, too poor to contribute money, but you can still labor earnestly in prayer. "The effective prayer of a righteous man can accomplish much" (James 5:16). Our hands are never tied when we can lift them up in prayer.

Prayer should be an essential part of any spiritual endeavor. If the church plans to have a gospel meeting, by all means, hand out flyers, invite your friends, schedule your attendance, but also pray! If the church decides to support a new evangelist, read his reports, contribute money toward his expenses, but also pray! If a sister is in surgery, visit her in the hospital, take a meal to her family, but also pray! If the church is thinking about appointing elders, ask questions and go through the process, but also pray and fast (Acts 14:23)! You may not be the speaker or the missionary or the surgeon or the elder-candidate, but your prayer is vital to secure the blessings of God. "Unless the Lord builds the house, they labor in vain who build it" (Psalm 127:1). Laboring in prayer is not sitting on the sidelines; it is playing on the field in a key position. Tangible work is pointless without behind-the-scenes diligence in prayer.

I know that I need to change my attitude about the worth of prayer. A normal day for me might be to go into the office and spend five minutes praying and five hours writing. What if I flipped those numbers? What if I spent five hours praying and sixty minutes writing? I probably would feel like I had not spent my time wisely. Yet, when Peter excused himself from serving tables, he said, "we will devote ourselves to prayer and to the ministry of the word" (Acts 6:4). Maybe if I spent more time praying, things would improve that I have failed to improve through studying, preaching, visiting, and cajoling. Paul planted, Apollos watered, "but God was causing the growth" (1 Corinthians 3:6).

Prayer is not an empty promise. When you say, "I'll be praying for you," follow up! Those prayers provide real results! Perhaps whole assemblies should be devoted to prayer, certainly at important moments, or when a member is facing major treatment, but even as a regular part of worship. Epaphras may seem like a minor character in the New Testament, but he made major contributions to the saints in Colossae, Laodicea, and Hierapolis, even from a long distance away. May God give us more who labor earnestly in prayer like Epaphras!

## Questions for Thought

1. Why doesn't prayer get the emphasis it deserves?

2. What are some characteristics of "laboring earnestly" in prayer?

3. What is your favorite example in Scripture of the effect of prayer?

4. What is your favorite example in your own life of the effect of prayer?

5. What are some ways to make your own private prayer time more effective? The congregation's prayer time?

# Onesiphorus:
## *Undaunted Supporter*

Of the books in the New Testament canon, 2 Timothy is likely the last letter Paul wrote. He composed it during his second lengthy Roman imprisonment.

The first time he was a Roman prisoner, he confidently stated, "I know that I will remain and continue on with you all for your progress and joy in the faith" (Philippians 1:25). Though the book of Acts ends before the verdict is handed down, historians are sure that Paul was acquitted and continued to journey throughout the Roman world preaching the gospel.

But this time, writing to Timothy, Paul seems to think his Roman imprisonment will end differently, and soon. He says:

> I am already being poured out as a drink offering, and the time of my departure has come. I have fought the good fight, I have finished the course, I have kept the faith; in the future there is laid up for me the crown of righteousness, which the Lord, the righteous Judge, will award to me on that day; and not only to me, but also to all who have loved His appearing (2 Timothy 4:6–8).

With Paul's execution bearing down, his relationships draw into sharp focus. He gives Timothy warnings concerning false brethren. He says, "You are aware of the fact that all who are in Asia turned away from me…" (2 Timothy 1:15). What loneliness Paul must have felt, having all his companions in Asia turn their backs on him, leaving him to face alone the difficulties of imprisonment and the specter of a Roman sword. Paul's persecutions had a way of revealing those who were his real friends, or more to the point, who were Jesus' real friends, those willing to risk their bodies and livelihoods for the sake of the gospel.

But Paul also mentions to Timothy the support he received from true brethren.

> The Lord grant mercy to the house of Onesiphorus, for he often re-freshed me and was not ashamed of my chains; but when he was in Rome, he eagerly searched for me and found me—the Lord grant to him to find mercy from the Lord on that day—and you know very well what services he rendered at Ephesus (2 Timothy 1:16–18).

Onesiphorus proved to be very different from the rest. He did not use Paul's imprisonment as an opportunity or excuse to abandon him. He helped Paul not once, and not just Paul, but rendered "services" in Ephesus multiple times.

Paul says that Onesiphorus "refreshed" him. Refreshment could refer to bringing Paul things needed for physical comfort—cloaks, blankets, ex-tra food and water—which were not usually provided by Roman captors. Refreshment could refer to companionship and conversation and prayer, things that would build up Paul's mind, spirit, and heart (Philemon 20) and allow him to carry on courageously. The roots of the name "Onesiphorus" actually mean "bringer of profit or advantage"; how fully Onesiphorus lived up to his name!

One deed in particular stands out. Onesiphorus was well-known in Ephesus, but at some point traveled to Rome—whether on business or specifically to minister to Paul, we cannot tell. Paul testifies that when he arrived, he "eagerly searched for me and found me." The way Paul phrases that leads me to think that he is drawing attention to Onesiphorus' stick-to-it-iveness.

There have been times that I've gone to visit a patient in the hospital, poked my head in the room, only to discover the patient was out for a test. If I were being honest, I would admit that occasionally a feeling of relief washes over me. I hastily scoot out so that I can hide out back at the office, without hav-ing to engage in messy conversation, or be brought down by the emotional burden of a person suffering and frail. I rationalize, "Well, I gave it a shot," or, "If they ask, I can say I tried," or, "Hey, it's the thought that counts." Sometimes I'll jot a note as proof that I showed up.

I must examine my heart! Onesiphorus' love for Paul was less selfish, more steadfast. He was no fair-weather friend. No delay or inconvenience or obstacle would prevent him from achieving his goal of building up the heart of Paul. I can only assume it was a much more daunting task to find Paul in the Roman prison system, than it is in our modern age of cars, computers, and ID numbers. It must have taken a lot of travel time, patience, prodding, and money. I would guess Onesiphorus encountered some false doors, uncooperative bureaucrats, pushy soldiers, and dead ends. There's meaning in the adverb—he didn't just search for Paul, he "eagerly" searched for Paul, with determination and expectation. He kept at it until he found him!

It wasn't just the logistical hassles that would have discouraged him. Being seen in the company of a notorious prisoner who was considered a public nuisance could have been very damaging to his reputation. If indeed Onesiphorus had any business dealings in Rome, they could be jeopardized. Why, just asking the wrong Roman soldier for access to Paul could have been dangerous. Onesiphorus didn't let that stop him. "He was not ashamed" of Paul's chains. Let's pray that, when the time comes, we have the same unashamed love for Jesus. "Everyone who confesses Me before men, I will also confess Him before My Father who is in heaven. But whoever denies Me before men, I will deny Him before My Father" (Matthew 10:32–33). That unashamed love is also demonstrated to Jesus when we extend it to His disciples.

> The King will say to those on His right, "Come, you who are blessed of My Father, inherit the kingdom prepared for you from the foundation of the world. For I was hungry, and you gave Me something to eat; I was thirsty, and you gave Me something to drink; I was a stranger, and you invited Me in; naked, and you clothed Me; I was sick, and you visited Me; I was in prison, and you came to Me."
> Then the righteous will answer Him, "Lord, when did we see

You hungry and feed You, or thirsty and give You something to drink? And when did we see You a stranger and invite You in, or naked and clothe You? When did we see You sick, or in prison, and come to You?"

The King will answer and say to them, "Truly I say to you, to the extent that you did it to one of these brothers of Mine, even the least of them, you did it to Me" (Matthew 25:34–40).

Since Paul greets the "household" of Onesiphorus (2 Timothy 4:19), it is possible that he had already passed away when Paul wrote this letter. While we understand that works do not earn salvation (Ephesians 2:8–9), Paul prays that Onesiphorus' deeds would be recompensed by an outpouring of God's mercy upon his household. Perhaps Paul was thinking of physical blessings—for the family to escape notice of Roman persecutors and be prosperous and successful. But since Paul says, "mercy from the Lord on that day," I tend to think he means eternal salvation.

Now, there is no comfort here for those who hope that philanthropy will cancel out entrenched immorality. Only repentance and the blood of Jesus answers for sin. But God sees His people's courage and good works, and often responds with mercy. That was the case with Ebed-melech the Ethiopian. In Jeremiah 38, the prophet Jeremiah preached that God's will was for the people to surrender the besieged city of Jerusalem and submit to Babylon. The king and his counselors put Jeremiah in a deep muddy cistern, where he was doomed to slowly sink and die. Ebed-melech heard what they had done and secured the king's permission to take thirty of his men and rescue Jeremiah. Later, in Jeremiah 39, God sent Jeremiah to give Ebed-melech the blessing of this message: "I am about to bring My words on this city for disaster and not for prosperity … But I will deliver you on that day … because you have trusted in Me …" (39:15–18). By our example, or by God's mercy, our faith helps our own families find salvation.

There is, in fact, a close relationship between helping others in the name of Christ and preparing our own souls for heaven. "Blessed are the merciful, for they shall receive mercy" (Matthew 5:7). "Judgment will be merciless to one who has shown no mercy; mercy triumphs over judgment" (James 2:13). "Behold, I am coming quickly, and My reward is with Me, to render to every man according to what he has done" (Revelation 22:12). May God grant us the courage to be loyal brothers, faithful servants, and tender-hearted supporters, and to let no obstacle or threat keep us from that goal. Recall Nehemiah's final words: "Remember me, O my God, for good!" (Nehemiah 13:31).

# Questions for Thought

1. How does Onesiphorus live up to his name?

2. After reading the last chapter, what do you suppose could be some manifestations of the cowardice condemned in Revelation 21:8?

3. What are some of the things that make good deeds difficult or inconvenient? Give an example of one time you failed to follow through.

4. Give an example of a time that a brother or sister in Christ sustained you by their arrival?

5. In what way do our good deeds anticipate our eternity?

# Philip:
## *Faithful in Four Phases*

AT VARIOUS POINTS IN Luke's account of the spread of the gospel through-out the Roman world, he mentions a man named Philip. This is not the Apostle Philip, but a Christian man who finds himself serving God in various capacities during thirty or more long years of ministry.

There is much to learn from this life well-lived, as Philip progresses from one ministry to the next. I have divided up his life into four distinct phases.

### Philip the Servant

We first meet Philip early in the history of the Jerusalem church.

> Now at this time while the disciples were increasing in number, a complaint arose on the part of the Hellenistic Jews against the native Hebrews, because their widows were being overlooked in the daily serving of food. So the twelve summoned the congregation of the disciples and said, "It is not desirable for us to neglect the word of God in order to serve tables. Therefore, brethren, select from among you seven men of good reputation, full of the Spirit and of wisdom, whom we may put in charge of this task. But we will devote ourselves to prayer and to the ministry of the word." The statement found approval with the whole congregation; and they chose Stephen, a man full of faith and of the Holy Spirit, and Philip, Prochorus, Nicanor, Timon, Parmenas, and Nicolas, a proselyte from Antioch. And these they brought before the apostles; and after praying, they laid their hands on them (Acts 6:1–6).

Greek-speaking Jewish widows needed to be fed, and the Apostles directed that seven men be selected from among the brethren who could be put in charge of the mundane but important task. The fact that it took seven men shows how much the church had grown! Philip was one of these men.

Luke does not use the noun *diakonos*, "deacon, servant," but he does use the related noun *diakonia*, "ministry," as well as the verb *diakoneo*, "to serve." Even if these men weren't given the title of deacon, they did the same sort of work. While their work may not have been glamorous, it was essential.

Philip was a man of humility, happy to wash feet. His service allowed the leaders to focus their attention on "prayer and the ministry of the word," the job that God Himself had given them. The phrase "not desirable" does not refer to Peter's own distaste for serving tables, but rather to God's assigning of talents and roles. The adjective *arestos* here means "acceptable, fit" (*Vine's; Please*, B1). It is not the best use of time and resources for teachers and shepherds to neglect spiritual work to mop floors and organize meals. It's not that Peter and the apostles were too snooty to do it, but it would have been inappropriate for them to spend too much time on it when they had a God-given ministry to fulfill.

Thus, Philip's service allowed the work of the whole church to move forward smoothly. It also helped him to prepare for greater works. As Paul would later say, "those who have served well as deacons obtain for themselves a high standing and great confidence in the faith that is in Christ Jesus" (1 Timothy 3:13).

### Philip the Teacher

In Acts 7 and 8, Saul attacked the Jerusalem church, emboldened after the stoning of Stephen.

> And on that day, a great persecution began against the church in Jerusalem, and they were all scattered throughout the regions of Judea and Samaria, except the apostles. Some devout men buried Stephen, and made loud lamentation over him. But Saul began ravaging the church, entering house after house, and dragging off men and women, he would put them in prison. Therefore, those who had been scattered went about preaching the word. Philip went down to the city of Samaria and began proclaiming Christ to them (Acts 8:1–5).

The disciples who scattered like dandelion seeds began to sprout and produce fruit in their new communities. Philip began preaching the gospel.

What a man of courage! Philip had been driven out of his home by persecution. He had watched one of his six fellow workers, Stephen, be stoned to death for his vocal faith. Rather than lay low and mind his own business for a bit, Philip immediately and bravely spoke up.

You may also remember that most of the Jews despised the Samaritans (John 8:48), who were interlopers who held to only a few portions of the Law and worshiped differently. Jesus had broken taboos by spending time in Samaritan lands and preaching to them (John 4:9; 4:40). Philip, too, extended to them the gospel.

Why do any of us wait? The Apostles stayed in Jerusalem, but Philip didn't need them at his shoulder to back him up. God Himself was backing him up. Why not this very week reach out to your neighbor, your friend, your cousin, your co-worker, with the good news of the gospel? Invite them to worship. Invite them to hear. Explain the reason for the hope that is in you (1 Peter 3:15). Don't be scared. Philip's boldness allowed him to convert many in the city, including the most famous man in town, Simon the Sorcerer (Acts 8:9–13). As a result, "there was much rejoicing in that city" (8:8).

### Philip the Evangelist

Soon, God gave Philip a new task. It's the same chapter, but I suggest there is a subtle shift in his work. In Samaria, he simply acted faithfully where he found himself. Now, God appointed him to carry the gospel to new territory.

> An angel of the Lord spoke to Philip saying, "Get up, and go south to the road that descends from Jerusalem to Gaza." (This is a desert road.) So he got up and went; and there was an Ethiopian eunuch, a court official of Candace, queen of the Ethiopians, who was in charge of all her treasure; and he had come to Jerusalem to worship,

and he was returning and sitting in his chariot, and was reading the prophet Isaiah. Then the Spirit said to Philip, "Go up and join this chariot" (Acts 8:26–29).

Philip introduced himself and offered to study with the eunuch. Philip used the passage in Isaiah to explain the gospel. "Beginning from this Scripture he preached Jesus to him" (8:35). This must have included not only who Jesus was and the salvation Jesus offered, but also how one should respond. Before long, the eunuch said, "Look! Water! What prevents me from being baptized?" (8:36) And they both went down into the water, and Philip baptized him into Jesus. I like to think that Philip's work started the evangelization of Egypt, Ethiopia, and all of northern Africa, as the newly-saved eunuch brought back the gospel with him to his homelands.

The eunuch wasn't Philip's only encounter.

> When they came up out of the water, the Spirit of the Lord snatched Philip away; and the eunuch no longer saw him, but went on his way rejoicing. But Philip found himself at Azotus, and as he passed through he kept preaching the gospel to all the cities until he came to Caesarea (Acts 8:39–40).

There were many coastal towns between Azotus and the large city of Caesarea, and Philip fulfilled his mission to speak the gospel in each one. The Lord needs more people who have the same "where-He-leads-I'll-follow" attitude. He needs people who spend the requisite time learning the Bible, so that they can go out as soldiers, planting the gospel into new hearts. He needs people who think of preaching not as a life of convenience, who do not search for "a good congregation," settling behind the protection of a padded pulpit in an established congregation, but who think of preaching as a life of service wherever God should lead.

### Philip the Father

I have saved the best for last. Luke says the least about this part of Philip's life. Nevertheless, if you were able to travel back in time and ask Philip, I would guess that this was the part that gave him the greatest sense of pride and satisfaction. It is Philip in his role as a father to four children. Luke tells the story of Paul's trip to Jerusalem, saying,

> On the next day we left and came to Caesarea, and entering the house of Philip the evangelist, who was one of the seven, we stayed with him. Now this man had four virgin daughters who were prophetesses (Acts 21:8–9).

It would seem that for about 25 years, Philip remained in Caesarea, sinking down roots and raising his family, preaching the gospel. And while reaching out to the community, he did not neglect reaching out to his own family. Much could be speculated about virgin daughters who were prophets, but it's safe to say that the girls were committed to righteousness in the midst of a sinful Greco-Roman society, and that they were busy and useful to the Lord in spreading the truth.

Let us never forget that the most important mission field is our own kitchen table. Let's be sure that we give our efforts to making sure that we save our own children, and give them the foundation they need to pass on the faith to their own children as well, so that when Jesus returns, the whole family will share a legacy of faith.

# Questions for Thought

1. How does serving in mundane roles prepare one for greater service to the Lord?


2. What changes about Philip's role between the beginning and end of Acts 8? What does not change?


3. What are some conclusions you draw about Christian life, after tracing Philip's life through about thirty years of his faith?


4. How can one balance various roles?


5. What are some of the important benefits of teaching the gospel to our own children?

# Tertius:
## *Scribe to Inspiration*

At the end of Paul's massive Roman letter, a new first-person voice breaks into the text.

> I, Tertius, who write this letter, greet you in the Lord (Romans 16:22).

In the ancient world, almost every letter was written through dictation. This was true whether the author was literate or illiterate, rich or poor, whether writing for business or personal reasons. A scribe, also called an amanuensis, would position himself at a table, while the author of the letter spoke the words to be written (see E. Randolph Richards, *Paul and First-Century Letter Writing: Secretaries, Composition, and Collection*).

Paul followed this convention when writing his inspired letters to churches. Paul himself only took up the pen at the end. Paul's personally handwritten section would serve to sign the letter. For example, in 2 Thessalonians 3:17–18:

> I, Paul, write this greeting with my own hand, and this is a distinguishing mark in every letter; this is the way I write. The grace of our Lord Jesus Christ be with you all.

Or Galatians 6:11 (and likely to the end of the chapter):

> See with what large letters I am writing to you with my own hand.

Paul's personal handwriting was one way a church could authenticate a letter as really coming from Paul. This would have been important when some forgeries were present (2 Thessalonians 2:2). Another way was to send it by the hand of a courier known to both Paul and the recipient (see Ephesians

6:21–22 and Colossians 4:7–9 for two examples).

Perhaps the autograph section also served as an opportunity for a personal touch. Like in 1 Corinthians 16:21–24:

> The greeting is in my own hand—Paul. If anyone does not love the Lord, he is to be accursed. Maranatha. The grace of the Lord Jesus be with you. My love be with you all in Christ Jesus. Amen.

Or the last verse of Colossians:

> I, Paul, write this greeting with my own hand. Remember my imprisonment. Grace be with you.

Or Philemon 19–20 (and likely more), where the autograph also serves as a guarantee of a promise to make good on any debts incurred by Onesimus:

> I, Paul, am writing this with my own hand, I will repay it (not to mention to you that you own to me even your own self as well). Yes, brother, let me benefit from you in the Lord; refresh my heart in Christ.

This practice is by no means limited to Paul's scribes. Silvanus (1 Peter 5:12) and Baruch (Jeremiah 36:27) are two other examples of amanuenses used by inspired authors. Many people also suggest that, because ancient letters were dictated orally, they were intended to be read aloud for fullest effect. Anyway, enough about the epistolary style of the ancient world. Back to Tertius!

Just think: all the amazing, inspired words that Paul wrote by the inspiration of the Holy Spirit, meant to instruct and uplift not only the Christians in Rome, but all Christians everywhere and for all time, were actually put to paper in neat rows by a man who is hidden almost entirely behind the scenes.

This is impressive to me. Tertius represents the hard work necessary to get the message of the gospel out to a lost and dying world, a link in the chain of evangelism which goes from the original inspired Apostles to today. Light a candle in a dark chamber, stand at a desk, dip quill into ink, and try to hand copy Romans; you'll see that it is a task neither quick nor easy!

Even today, a lot of effort must be exerted to broadcast the gospel throughout any community. Perhaps a person doesn't have the ability or opportunity to preach. But that person can help lay out the bulletin. He or she can run photocopies of tracts for the foyer or collate and staple teaching material for the kids' classes. One can build a website for the church to post sermons and articles and keep it up to date. One can spread advertisements on social media or pass out flyers hand to hand.

Information doesn't have to be in written form to qualify as sharing the word. In John 4, the Samaritan woman at the well had a discussion with Jesus and became convinced that He was in fact the Christ.

> So the woman left her waterpot, and went into the city and said to the men, "Come, see a man who told me all the things that I have done; this is not the Christ, is it?" They went out of the city and were coming to Him. … From that city, many of the Samaritans believed in Him because of the word of the woman who testified, "He told me all the things that I have done." … And they were saying to the woman, "It is no longer because of what you said that we believe, for we have heard for ourselves and know that this One is indeed the Savior of the world" (John 4:28–30, 39, 42).

In like manner today, the gospel preacher likely has only a limited circle of acquaintances, a great percentage of which tends to be members of the church already. Effective evangelism happens when all the members of the congregation invite their friends, neighbors, family members, and acquaintances, to come and hear the gospel preached.

Tertius was not inspired. But without Tertius' work, we wouldn't have Paul's inspired letter to the Romans in our Bibles. And the gospel finds its way into hearts and minds today through the faithful work of non-inspired folks who pass along the inspired word.

## Questions for Thought

1. What was the role of the ancient amanuensis?

2. Give some reasons why the presence of an amanuensis should not challenge our notion of the verbal inspiration of the New Testament.

3. Where would the Roman letter be without Tertius?

4. How can you help the preacher and elders of your congregation get the truth into the hands and the minds of people in the community?

# Lydia:
## *Great Faith in Small Places*

EARLY ON PAUL'S SECOND MISSIONARY JOURNEY, he revisited the cities where he had previously planted the gospel, bringing news from the Jerusalem discussion, and strengthening the churches there (Acts 16:1–5). But, the Spirit of God would not allow Paul and his traveling companions to spend much time in those areas, being steadily forced west to Troas and the shore of the Aegean Sea. Finally, the Spirit reveals why:

> A vision appeared to Paul in the night: a certain man of Macedonia was standing and appealing to him, and saying, "Come over to Macedonia and help us." And when he had seen the vision, immediately we sought to go into Macedonia, concluding that God had called us to preach the gospel to them.
>
> Therefore, putting out to sea from Troas, we ran a straight course to Samothrace, and on the day following to Neapolis; and from there to Philippi, which is a leading city of the district of Macedonia, a Roman colony; and we were staying in this city for some days (Acts 16:9–12).

Clearly, God felt that it was time for Paul to push the gospel message even farther west, into lands reached by boat across the Aegean: European lands such as Macedonia and Greece.

It doesn't take long for the first convert to be identified.

> On the Sabbath day, we went outside the gate to a riverside, where we were supposing that there would be a place of prayer; and we sat down and began speaking to the women who had assembled. And a certain woman named Lydia, from the city of Thyatira, a seller of purple fabrics, a worshiper of God, was listening; and the Lord opened her heart to respond to the things spoken by Paul. And

when she and her household had been baptized, she urged us, saying, "If you have judged me to be faithful to the Lord, come into my house and stay." And she prevailed upon us (Acts 16:13–15).

I find at least four lessons from Paul's encounter with Lydia.

**Never Ignore or Underestimate Anyone.**
Look carefully at the details of the Macedonian call. If I were Paul, I would likely be keeping my eyes open for a person fitting the description of the man in the vision. At least, I would be expecting that God would lead me first to preach to a "certain man of Macedonia." But it turns out that God led him first to preach to a certain woman of Asia, from a city near Troas where Paul had recently sailed!

Philippi was a Roman colony that would have offered many opportunities to speak to soldiers and government officials and Gentile idolaters. But Paul's first audience was not in the marketplace, or in a hall of philosophy. Instead, since there was not even a Jewish synagogue in town, he went down to a stream, to find a prayer meeting of Jewish women.

One of my guiltiest memories is being on a plane, when the person next to me was talkative and annoying. I just wanted to bury my face in the book I planned to read and be left alone! What if that had been a God-given opportunity? Had I been more responsive, and more mindful of the needs of a lost and dying world, I could have shared the gospel (and if he had thought me talkative and annoying, serves him right). God presents us all kinds of riverside opportunities; we just need to get better at recognizing them for what they are. Keep your eyes open and your Bible with you! Take out your earbuds and interact with the people around you! I'm grateful Paul did not turn up his nose at a meeting of women by the riverside and move on to bigger things.

An ancient prophet, speaking of the tiny remnant of God's people, and the unimpressive foundation of God's second temple, cautioned, "Who has despised the day of small things?" (Zechariah 4:10). Let us never forget that, all around us at this very instant, there are opportunities to preach the gospel to people who would respond, if they could only hear. We have just overlooked them thus far. We don't need to book a concert hall to preach the gospel; we can start with the grocery store clerk or the mail carrier or our neighbor.

**Diligent Faith Is Often Rewarded.**
Louis Pasteur once said, "Fortune favors the prepared mind." He meant that what looks like a lucky discovery is due to years of study and searching. In a similar way, God's grace is often received by those looking for it.

Let's consider Lydia for a moment. The phrase "a worshiper of God" is almost always a technical term for either a Jewish proselyte, or a Gentile who is interested and perhaps attends synagogue (see Acts 10:2; 13:43 "God-fearing proselytes," 17:4 "God-fearing Greeks"). We can safely assume that Lydia was a Gentile convert to Judaism.

She was a *porphyropolis,* a fabric seller traveling on business, whose main home was in Thyatira, a town renown for the purple dye of the murex shell. It's not hard to assume certain impediments to her worshiping God. She could have focused on her business. Undoubtedly the other merchants were open in the marketplace that day, scooping up her sales. Time is money. Plus, it was probably disheartening that there was no real synagogue in town—a feeling I've sometimes had while on vacation when finding a group of five or ten Christians to worship with. Why bother at all?

What great faith Lydia showed in unfavorable circumstances, to take the time to pause and observe the Sabbath and join herself with whatever little group was meeting to pray and read. Those who make time for worship often find they receive a greater blessing than they expected! Because she came, she heard the gospel. I don't believe for a moment this was a chance encounter. God heard her prayers, as clearly as He heard Cornelius praying devoutly and saw the Ethiopian reading his scroll and sent Paul the messenger.

**God Opens Hearts to Respond to the Word.**

For good reason, we usually focus on the "sinner's part" in salvation. There's no question that the gospel is an imperative and that a person hearing the gospel must believe and respond. When one hears the gospel, one must "obey" (John 3:36) there is something he must "do" (Acts 2:37; 9:6; 16:30; etc.) to receive the promised blessings, including being baptized. God will not overrule a person's will; the Holy Spirit can be resisted (Acts 7:51). I stand by the conviction that Calvinism completely misunderstands the role of man in God's plan of salvation. Being saved is not a passive process. When the word, "the power of God for salvation," enters his mind, a person doesn't wait to see what God will do next; instead, he leaps at the opportunity to be saved!

But we go too far if we believe that God is absent from this process. There is no need to hide from Acts 16:14, "the Lord opened her heart to respond to the things spoken by Paul." The word *prosecho* may be translated "give heed" rather than "respond," as it is in KJV. *Vine's Dictionary* (Give, #16; Attend, #1) says, "to turn one's mind to, attend to." Compare other verses where this word appears, such as "giving attention" in Acts 8:6, and "pay attention" in 1 Timothy 1:4; 4:1; Titus 1:14; Hebrews 2:1. It may be that God is opening her heart to listen, which is less forceful an idea than grabbing her by the neck and compelling her to be saved. The New Testament does not teach that God overrides the human conscience.

Let us pray that God will "open doors" for the gospel to be preached (Colossians 4:3). God will often bring together a seeker and a preacher, if both are diligent. Let us pray that God will grant wisdom (James 1:5). Let us pray for God to touch the hearts of individual people with whom we are studying (Romans 10:1). We must plant and water, but God gives the increase (1 Corinthians 3:6). When someone is particularly closed-minded to the gospel, let us pray that God will send the kind of circumstances that will cause him to focus on spiritual things.

It's not that God forced Lydia to believe. God created the plan, bent the course of human history, sent the Christ in the fullness of time, gave His

Son as a sacrificial gift, and broadcast the truth. For Lydia personally, God opened the doors, provided the right circumstances, sent her the preacher, and removed the obstacles, to help her respond to the word. When Lydia stands before God, she will not smugly pat herself on the back and remember how she achieved salvation, but will collapse in unending thanksgiving that God secured, recorded, and communicated salvation to her! We do not congratulate ourselves for obeying; we thank God for providing. As Paul later wrote to the same Philippians, "I thank my God in all my remembrance of you … confident of this very thing, that He who began a good work in you, will perfect it until the day of Christ Jesus" (Philippians 1:3–6).

**Get Involved Right Away.**
Lydia immediately put her new-found faith in Jesus to work. She brought the evangelists to her home to speak to her "household" and they were converted to Christ. She opened her home to the evangelists to use it as a base of operations. Perhaps she was wealthy enough from sale of purple to have a big home. Apparently, her home soon became the meeting place for the church, for it is there that Paul and Silas returned after their arrest, where they "saw the brethren … encouraged them and departed" (Acts 16:40).

We can only guess how many disciples Paul made in Philippi before pressing on to Thessalonica. But we do know that when he writes his letter to the Philippian church (maybe 8–10 years later), its tone is extremely positive, and it is addressed to a very active and faithful congregation. In fact, it was one of the few congregations that supported Paul's work elsewhere in the region (Philippians 4:15–19). Surely, Lydia's instant and ongoing work had a big hand in the success of the gospel in Philippi.

# Questions for Thought

1.  What brought Paul to Philippi?

2.  In what unassuming location did Paul first find faith in all of Europe?

3.  What circumstances could have caused Lydia to miss out?

4.  In what way did God work on Lydia's heart? What did Lydia still have to do?

5.  How long did Lydia wait before putting her new faith to work?

# Manaen:
## *Radical Change*

THERE IS A PHENOMENON IN SCIENCE called "sensitive dependence on initial conditions in a dynamical system," more commonly known as "the butterfly effect."

In 1951, a meteorologist named Edward Lorenz was using a computer to run a model of weather predictions. The first time, he entered a value of 0.506127 for one of the mathematical variables in the model, the most digits the primitive computer would hold. The next time, Lorenz took a shortcut and only carried out the variable to the thousandths place, 0.506.

We're talking about a truly tiny change. It's like buying a $1,000 car in cash and discovering you're missing a dime. It's like filling a gallon jug and coming up nine drops of water short. It's a negligible, meaningless amount, and you wouldn't give it a moment's thought. Thus, Lorenz was stunned to discover that when he ran the model the second time, the computer came up with a completely different weather prediction!

If this seems preposterous, let us remember that, depending on the seller, one dime could be the difference between your walking home and driving home.

Realizing that the miniscule change in just one variable could have gigantic results in outcomes, Lorenz published his findings in a paper for the New York Academy of Sciences, and stated, "One flap of a seagull's wings could change the course of weather forever." In later papers and speeches, he changed the seagull to a nicer-sounding butterfly, and a new phrase was coined that has found its way into popular culture.

The "butterfly effect" can be seen in situations where two objects begin close together but end up very far apart. If you've ever watched the Plinko carnival game, you know that discs can be placed in the same top slot, but will bounce slightly differently off pegs on the way down, and may land on opposite sides of the board. In like manner, the Eastern Continental Divide runs through the field just west of the church building where I worship. If I stand on the ridge, face north and spit over my left shoulder, it'll roll westward, join the Caloosahatchee, and eventually reach the Gulf of Mexico. If I spit over my right shoulder, it'll roll eastward, join the Kissimmee, and eventually reach the Atlantic Ocean. A change in a few inches in starting position results in a change in hundreds of miles in end position.

By now you must be asking why any of this matters, and who is this guy Manaen from the title. In Acts 13:1, we are introduced to the teachers and prophets at the church in Antioch:

> Barnabas, and Simeon who was called Niger, and Lucius of Cyrene, and Manaen who had been brought up with Herod the tetrarch, and Saul.

From this point Luke begins to describe the exciting and important missionary work of Paul and Barnabas, and we forget about once-mentioned Manaen. But this description of him is truly fascinating, and it deserves our closer attention.

The Herod to whom Luke refers is Herod Antipas, one of the most corrupt, sinful individuals mentioned in Scripture. His father was Herod the Great, the so-called king of Judea who slaughtered the infants in Bethlehem in an effort to destroy Jesus. Herod Antipas was tetrarch of Galilee and Perea until 39 AD. He is the Herod who stole his brother's wife and beheaded John the Baptist (Mark 6:14–29). He is the Herod who mocked Jesus and sent Him back to Pilate (Luke 23:8–12). His nephew, Herod Agrippa, is the one who killed James in Acts 12:1–2. Obviously, the Herods were not nice people.

While the Greek term for "brought up with," *syntrophos,* could mean a number of things, including "attendant at court," all the translations except the RSV prefer the most natural meaning, "childhood companion, or foster brother," from the verb *trepho,* "to bring up or raise" (see Luke 4:16) and the prefix *syn,* "with or together." Some scholars believe that the two had been nursed together and raised together by the same woman (McGarvey, *Commentary on Acts,* Vol. 2, p. 2).

Whatever the precise details of their childhood, it is clear that Herod Antipas and Manaen started out in similar circumstances and in the same household. Their masters taught them the same lessons, gave them same privileges, and pointed them toward the same goals. They witnessed the same sights and heard the same sounds. They may have eaten at the same tables and reclined on the same cushions. It is therefore utterly amazing that one went on to become a hedonistic pagan and murderous tyrant, and the other went on to become a follower of Jesus Christ and a teacher of the gospel!

When I was a kid, my family spent the summers in a trailer in the back-woods of central New York state. Without cell phones, nature was our playground. We spent many afternoons adventuring in a rocky creek near the trailer. One game consisted of putting two identical sticks side by side in the stream, then giving chase as the stream carried them off. Before long, an eddy would catch one just a little more than the other, and send it off at a slightly different angle. It would then bump a rock that the other would miss completely, and they would drift apart. By the time we could no longer keep up with them, they were often on completely different sides of the stream, yards and yards apart. One imagines they emerged into the ocean separated by days.

Herod and Manaen were two sticks placed into the same stream, but they ended up in very different places. This is an imperfect metaphor. The sticks' separation was caused by random waves or a lucky bounce. Herod and Manaen's separation was caused by the way these two men chose to respond to the ever-present call of the gospel.

Is it possible for a person steeped in a sinful environment, fed on the phi-losophies of evolution and materialism, saturated in the ways of the society, to chart a different course from his peers? Yes! Is it possible for a person attending a lousy high school to choose to swim against the culture? Yes! Is it possible for one member of godless and wretched household to become a Christian? Yes! The amazing power of the gospel is that it can resonate in the hearts of a few sensitive individuals, and cause them to separate from the world.

How did two people, Manaen and Herod Antipas, start so similarly, and finish so differently? Because they received differently the truth of the gospel. Their eternal abodes will be very different, forever different.

The Bible says, "Do not be conformed to this world, but be transformed by the renewing of your mind, that you may prove what the will of God is, that which is good and acceptable and perfect" (Romans 12:1–2). Beware, because the same "butterfly effect" can be observed in the church building, too. Two men may sit in the same pew, hear the same sermons, sing the same songs—one can strive for eternal life, the other can turn a deaf ear. Two sisters can attend the same Bible classes and grow up in the same wholesome household—one can put God first, the other reject God entirely.

What starts together doesn't have to stay together, thanks to the transformative power of the gospel.

## Questions for Thought

1. Who was the Herod of Acts 13:1?


2. What was Manaen's place in Herod's household?

3.  Can you think of another biblical example of a person who ended up in a very different place than where he started?

4.  What are some of the things that influence people to go in different directions? How can one thing influence two people differently?

5.  How does this study change your approach to evangelizing the community?

# Apollos:
## *A Ten-Talent Man*

Luke introduces us to Apollos in Acts 18:24–28.

> A Jew named Apollos, an Alexandrian by birth, an eloquent man,
> came to Ephesus; and he was mighty in the Scriptures. This man
> had been instructed in the way of the Lord; and being fervent in
> spirit, he was speaking and teaching accurately the things concern-
> ing Jesus, being acquainted only with the baptism of John; and he
> began to speak out boldly in the synagogue. But when Priscilla and
> Aquila heard him, they took him aside and explained to him the
> way of God more accurately. And when he wanted to go across to
> Achaia, the brethren encouraged him and wrote to the disciples to
> welcome him; and when he had arrived, he greatly helped those
> who had believed through grace, for he powerfully refuted the Jews
> in public, demonstrating by the Scriptures that Jesus was the Christ.

Most of Jesus' early disciples were uneducated men from the Galilean coun-
tryside (Acts 4:13), though this did not stop them from being very effective
in spreading the truth. As the gospel spread throughout the Greco-Roman
world, it would seem that, generally speaking, most converts came from the
lower classes.

> Consider your calling, brethren, that there were not many wise
> according to the flesh, not many mighty, not many noble; but
> God has chosen the foolish things of the world to shame the wise
> (1 Corinthians 1:26–29).

Apollos was one of the exceptions, a man who came from a promising background. He was born and raised in Alexandria, one of the wealthiest, most
cosmopolitan and sophisticated cities on the planet, a place where Jewish
learning and Greek culture often mingled.

The standing of Alexandria in the first century cannot be overstated. It vied with Rome for title of largest city in the world, and with Athens for title of most learned. It had been founded by Alexander the Great 300 years previously, to control the supply routes through Egypt; but it was also designed from scratch—even the layout of the building and streets—to be a beacon of Hellenized culture. It was the home of the famous Library of Alexandria, and a great Museum in the classical sense, a "home of the muses," a place for musicians, poets, and philosophers to study and perform. Seventy rabbis in Alexandria produced the Septuagint version of the Scriptures, a Greek translation of the Old Testament that circulated throughout the world and was frequently quoted by New Testament authors.

It seems that Apollos made the most of the opportunities afforded to him in Alexandria. He was "mighty in the Scriptures," which suggests he had a powerful mind able to grasp and retain a lot from the books of the Old Testament. He obviously devoted himself to hours of reading and study. He was "eloquent," which suggests that he possessed the natural gift of charisma, and he polished his ability to present the truth publicly to an audience. He was "fervent in spirit," which suggests that he made it his passion and work to speak openly to people wherever and whenever he met them. He later "powerfully refuted the Jews in public," which suggests that he knew the tools of rhetoric to persuasively argue his point.

Somehow, sometime, perhaps through evangelists coming to Alexandria, or perhaps through his own trips to Jerusalem, Apollos came by news of the ministry of Jesus. Some think he even may have been a disciple of John the Baptist before or during Jesus' ministry, though that seems unlikely to me. In any case, once he realized that Jesus was indeed the Christ promised in the Old Testament, he began proclaiming the truth of the gospel. When we first meet him in Acts 18, he had come to Ephesus of Asia, "speaking out boldly in the synagogue."

Apollos was smart and capable and confident. He was the proverbial ten-talent man. But here's the thing: the world has no shortage of people God has given intelligence and ability and opportunity, but who do not have a renewed heart and devotion to Jesus; who squander their talents, or worse, use them to support the domain of darkness. There are plenty of atheists with a 1600 on their SATs. There are plenty of wise, beautiful, talented progressives. Thanks be to God that Apollos' great learning did not make him too smug for Christ.

Furthermore, thanks be to God that Apollos used his talents primarily for spreading the good news of Jesus. He decided that nothing else was as worth his time and effort. He could have devoted his life to becoming his generation's greatest lawyer, he could have convinced large crowds to pay money to sit at his feet and soak up his great learning. Instead, he preached Jesus. Preachers today must realize that time spent convincing others to vote for particular candidates is time spent less fruitfully. You may convince many to vote Republican, but we don't need a bunch of unsaved Republicans, we need a bunch of Christians. You may get people to finally agree with you that increased taxation is immoral, but what good is that unless they confess that Jesus is the Christ? Don't waste your emotional capital on politics—if you're going to get in a heated argument, make it a worthwhile one—argue about the person of Jesus. "Make the most of your time" and your talents (Ephesians 5:16).

In Ephesus, Apollos was "teaching accurately the things concerning Jesus." Well, mostly. There was a hole in his knowledge concerning baptism into Jesus. As Paul's subsequent encounter with some disciples in Ephesus shows, it was a big enough deficiency to require Paul to preach on baptism and "re"-baptize those disciples (Acts 19:1–7).

By the way, this has always struck me as indicative of how important is the "one baptism" of the New Testament (Ephesians 4:4–7). The baptism of John was perfectly valid before the death of Jesus; but once Jesus shed His blood and took His place at the Father's right hand, only baptism into Christ will do for salvation. There's not a whole lot of difference between John's baptism and baptism into Jesus. Imagine: if you stood out of earshot and observed Apollos baptizing with John's baptism, and Paul baptizing into Jesus, they would look identical. They featured the same object: penitent believers. They baptized into in the same medium: water. They baptized in the same way: immersion. The only difference is the intangible purpose of the two: one pointed to Christ, the other was into Christ. For this reason, when members of the Baptist church speak of baptism in recognition that one has already been saved, I must argue that this is not the one baptism of New Testament scripture. Baptism into Christ is *in order to be* saved (see Romans 6:3-6; 1 Peter 3:21; Acts 22:16). If the purpose is different, this is enough to ask someone to be "re-baptized;" or strictly speaking, to be baptized actually and truly into the name of Jesus Christ, in the way that He has commanded.

Back to Apollos. That he was educated and eloquent doesn't mean he was snooty. In the first place, he possessed the humility to confess his need for a Savior, and submit himself to a crucified Christ. He died to self and took up the cross! But moreover, in Ephesus, he demonstrated the willingness to learn from the meek and lowly. Priscilla and Aquila hailed from frontier lands near the Black Sea (Acts 18:2), and surely did not have the opportunities for education Apollos had. But they understood the truth better than he did on the subject of baptism. When they "took him aside and explained to him the way of God more accurately," he listened to their arguments, consulted the Scriptures, and changed his doctrine. Big shot preachers holding a fancy college degree and wearing a suit ought never dismiss the wisdom and biblical insight of plain country folk holding a shovel and wearing suspenders.

Apollos, with enthusiasm to share his new knowledge, continued preaching. He worked hard in Ephesus, even to reason with and to "powerfully refute in public" the Jews who refused to see Christ in the Scripture. For this and other reasons, some commentators such as Luther suggest that maybe Apollos is the author of the book of Hebrews—though this seems a stretch to me. Eventually, Apollos crossed the Aegean Sea to preach in Corinth (Acts 19:1), where he watered the seed that Paul had earlier planted. In fact, some liked his preaching so much they started factions, which horrified Paul as well as Apollos, who was with Paul (according to 1 Corinthians 16:12) as he wrote this rebuke:

Now I mean this, that each one of you is saying, "I am of Paul," and
"I of Apollos," and "I of Cephas," and "I of Christ." Has Christ been
divided? Paul was not crucified for you, was he? … What then is
Apollos? And what is Paul? Servants through whom you believed,
even as the Lord gave opportunity to each one. I planted, Apollos
watered, but God was causing the growth… (1 Corinthians 1:12,
13; 3:4–6; see 3:22; 4:6).

We all must be especially careful never to become infected with "preacheritis." It's a wonderful thing to be taught week to week by a guy who is easy
to listen to. I will drive two hours to attend a Bible lecture given by one of
a handful of my "favorite" preachers. But if the membership of a congregation declines because a popular preacher moves, we have misunderstood
the meaning and responsibilities of being a member of the church. There's
nothing wrong with working hard to become an effective communicator in
the pulpit and from house to house, nor the leaders of a church asking such
a person to work with their congregation; in fact, there's everything right
with it! But members must stop basing their attendance and contributions
and faith on any human being. We must not lose touch with the One we are
really worshiping and serving.

God continued to use Apollos for many years. In 1 Corinthians 16:12,
he headed to other cities to preach. In Titus 3:13, he headed to Crete.
Undoubtedly, he used his learning, boldness, and eloquence not to attract
followers to himself, but to save souls for Jesus.

It takes all kinds. Some minister to college kids, some to drug addicts. Some
preach to big wealthy congregations, some to small poor congregations.
Some teach Greek grammar, some leave the lexicons on the shelf, and focus on sharing the truth with the meek and lowly. Some preach Evidences,
some John 3:16. The brotherhood needs the expertise of Apollos, but it
needs the diligence of all. Find your place in the kingdom of God and contribute your own special talents to the best of your ability!

# Questions for Thought

1. In what way was Apollos' background different from most of the apostles?

2. Did this hinder him from being an effective evangelist?

3. Who corrected Apollos' doctrine? How did they do it without causing offense?

4. What are some features of the one baptism of the New Testament?

5. An early case of "preacheritis" seems to have taken hold in Corinth (1 Corinthians 1:12). How can Christians appreciate good preaching without becoming distracted groupies?

# Euodia and Syntyche:
## *Harmony in the Church*

PAUL'S LETTER TO THE SAINTS AT Philippi is his most upbeat letter. He constantly thanks them for their love and support, and repeatedly praises them for their exemplary behavior and diligent efforts at spreading the gospel. He calls them, "my joy and crown" (4:1). There is almost nothing in the whole letter that could be viewed as negative.

Well, almost.

> I urge Euodia and I urge Syntyche to live in harmony in the Lord. Indeed, true companion, I ask you also to help these women who have shared my struggle in the cause of the gospel, together with Clement also and the rest of my fellow workers, whose names are in the book of life (Philippians 4:2–3).

Two otherwise wonderful women in the Philippian congregation were not getting along. The issue doesn't appear to have been related to any false teaching or any terrible immorality; if it were, Paul surely would have commanded one or both to repent. Nevertheless, the dispute was bad enough, or had been going on long enough, that Paul brought it up. He asked them to "live in harmony."

Anytime there is rancor in the church, there is a problem. Christians are called to treat one another as members of a loving family. Paul commands:

> …walk in a manner worthy of the calling with which you have been called, with all humility and gentleness, with patience, showing tolerance for one another in love, being diligent to preserve the unity of the Spirit in the bond of peace (Ephesians 4:1–3).

Furthermore,

> Let all bitterness and wrath and anger and clamor and slander be
> put away from you, along with all malice. Be kind to one another,
> tender-hearted, forgiving each other, just as God in Christ also has
> forgiven you (Ephesians 4:31–32).

Because the church is made of people dwelling in close proximity, there will inevitably be friction and pain. Someone will give someone else reason to get upset, sometimes on accident, sometimes on purpose. Someone will take someone else's pew. Someone will leave someone else out of a pot-luck invitation. Someone will forget to pay a debt, or scream a put-down. Someone will gossip, steal $20, or commit adultery. It's how Christians deal with these mistakes and misunderstandings, these insults and attacks, that allow the church to live up to its calling and shine forth the image of Jesus.

A sudden upwelling of anger is one thing (Ephesians 4:26). But lingering resentment or malice is not an option. "If you bite and devour one another, take care that you are not consumed by one another" (Galatians 5:15). Rancor in the assembly makes it hard to worship. Jesus points out that reconciliation is important for good worship (Matthew 5:23-24). In fact, when brethren can't resolve their issues and get along, it suggests to the world that the gospel has no power to change the heart, no peace to offer (John 17:21).

But it seemed especially dispiriting here, in Philippi, because Euodia and Syntyche were no fringe members. They were active in the ministry. They shared Paul's struggle in the cause of spreading the gospel. Paul should have been able to offer a thankful greeting, recognizing their great service and accomplishments, but instead he has to besmirch his greeting to them by drawing attention to their squabble.

Note that Paul doesn't pick sides nor assign blame. His purposeful repetition of the verb before both names—"I urge Euodia and I urge Syntyche"—emphasizes the need for both women to do something to foster reconciliation. When it comes to man's estrangement from God, the fault of the division is always totally ours. God justly says, "Return to Me, that I may return to you" (Zechariah 1:3). However, when it comes to two human beings' estrangement from one another, it's almost always the case that both people have fault to bear, and should take some steps to apologize and meet in the middle.

Paul also notes that their names are recorded in the book of life, which of course is a metaphor for their salvation (see Revelation 20:11–15). Paul doesn't do this just to help the medicine go down with a spoonful of sugar, nor to downplay the effect of their squabble. Two people bound for the same Heaven should have every motivation to live in harmony. Thoughts of Heaven have a way of reminding us that earthly things are temporary and meaningless. Two people bound for the same Heaven should possess every skill for coming to terms granting forgiveness. Every one of the fruit of the spirit—"love, joy, peace, patience, kindness, goodness, faithfulness, gentleness, self-control" (Galatians 5:22–23)—is an attitude or action that, among other things, makes harmony among believers possible.

Jesus challenged His disciples,

> A new commandment I give to you, that you love one another, even as I have loved you, that you also love one another. By this all men will know that you are My disciples, if you have love for one another (John 13:34–35.)

One might wonder what's so new about this so-called "new commandment." After all, it's not like Jesus is the first person who commanded love. The word "love" appears in the Old Testament over 130 times, and God's attribute of "lovingkindness" over 175 times. When Jesus spoke the Golden Rule in Matthew 7:12, He echoed Leviticus 19:18, "you shall love your neighbor as yourself." Even avoiding vengeance and loving enemies is an Old Testament ethic (Leviticus 19:17, 34; Deuteronomy 10:19; Proverbs 24:17; 25:21–22). The "new commandment" is not new because love is a new concept, but because the degree to which it was to be shown was fully demonstrated in Jesus. We are to love others "even as I have loved you."

Jesus demonstrated His love by dying on the cross (Matthew 20:20–28; Luke 23:34; John 15:13)! "Therefore be imitators of God, as beloved children; and walk in love, just as Christ also loved you, and gave Himself up for us, an offering and a sacrifice to God" (Ephesians 5:1–2). Clearly, when we gain the right perspective, there's little in this world that can prevent us from overcoming our injured feelings and patiently addressing our genuine complaints.

What does this new selfless love look like in action? Paul provides a glimpse:

> Love is patient, love is kind and is not jealous; love does not brag and is not arrogant, does not act unbecomingly; it does not seek its own, is not provoked, does not take into account a wrong suffered, does not rejoice in unrighteousness, but rejoices with the truth; bears all things, believes all things, hopes all things, endures all things (1 Corinthians 13:4–7).

True Christian love always has others' best interests in mind. If our behavior followed this pattern at all times, our relationships would climb upward in a spiral of mutual goodness.

Now, if rancor between two Christians is loud enough, or goes on long enough without a resolution, perhaps it's time to bring in a third party to help. A good example of this is 1 Corinthians 1:11, in which "Chloe's people" inform Paul of the problems at Corinth. By the way, this is not gossip. Chloe's intentions were not to sully or demean, but to help. I am confident she said something to those involved first (Matthew 18:15–17), and when they wouldn't budge, openly turned to Paul.

In that same spirit, Paul asks a certain *suzugos* to help these women resolve their differences and get back to the work of the Lord. All major translations take *suzugos* as an unnamed person who is a true "companion" or "yokefellow" to Paul. But it is very possible that it should be taken as a proper name, a man named Suzugos, whose name was "true" because Paul had come to rely on his companionship. Don't think this odd—just so, Onesimus was aptly named "Useful" (Philemon 10–11), and Joseph received the name Barnabas, meaning "Son of Encouragement" (Acts 4:36).

How can a third party help?

- Most of the time, just keep your nose out of other people's business (Proverbs 26:17; Luke 12:13). It's not pretty and it's probably not righteous, but sometimes even purebreds have to growl and snap for a few seconds. They will work it out.
- When it becomes clear that lasting peace is at stake—when people are moving their seats in the pews, when people are refusing to attend potlucks in certain members' homes, when people are taking their names off the worship duty list and class teacher list—it's time to speak up.
- Mention your concern that the squabble is starting to disturb and even damage the church. Speak gently. "The tongue of the wise brings healing" (Proverbs 12:18). "The mouth of the righteous is a fountain of life" (Proverbs 10:11). "A man has joy in an apt answer, and how delightful is a timely word" (Proverbs 15:23).
- Offer to sit down with both parties as a peacemaker and mediator. "A man's counsel is sweet to his friend" (Proverbs 27:9). Or suggest they sit down with a dispassionate elder or wise Christian who has the trust and respect of both parties (1 Corinthians 6:5).
- Avoid picking sides. Remember that Satan is the enemy here not the people (2 Timothy 2:24–26) and division is his desire.
- Never gossip. "He who covers a transgression seeks love, but he who repeats a matter separates intimate friends" (Proverbs 17:9; cf. 11:3).
- Pray for them (Colossians 1:9–12).
- Remind them what is at stake; it's better to be defrauded than to let the church suffer injury (1 Corinthians 6:7).
- Sadly, some disagreements must end with a split (Acts 15:37–40) at least for a while. If the conflict cannot be resolved, perhaps it's time for someone to move for the sake of peace.

What does it take for Christians to "live in harmony in the Lord"? I don't suppose we have to see eye to eye on every little thing. But we should remember we are part of the same family. "Greet the friends by name" (3 John 15). Squabblers could simply put on a sweet face, but Christ expects us to actually fix our problems. We should learn to be generous to a fault (Matthew 5:42), involved in acts of goodness (Matthew 25:34–40) and able to forgive without limit (Matthew 18:22). Failing to reconcile after a reasonable period of time stops being a distraction and starts flirting with sin (Matthew 5:24; 1 Corinthians 3:3).

Modern day Euodias and Syntyches need to get over it and patch it up, and return to the wonderful work of building up the church and saving souls. Lack of harmony will distract or even cripple a church. Disharmony makes outsiders doubt the power of the gospel, if brethren can't solve their problems with love.

# Questions for Thought

1. What are some situations that can cause misunderstandings or friction of the sort that Euodia and Syntyche had?

2. What is especially sad about Euodia and Syntyche's squabble?

3. Which phrase from Paul's description of love in 1 Corinthians 13 is most meaningful to you? Describe one specific situation in which it can be shown.

4. When is the best time for a concerned friend to get involved in a squabble? Why was the action of Chloe's people *not* gossip?

5. Describe a time you got involved and it proved helpful. Describe a time you got involved and it didn't go well, and what you learned for next time.

# Barnabas:
## *Son of Encouragement*

THERE ARE MANY JOSEPHS IN THE BIBLE, but one earns a stand-out nickname. In Acts 4:36 Luke introduces us to

> Joseph, a Levite of Cyprian birth, who was also called Barnabas by the apostles (which translated means Son of Encouragement).

Throughout his life of ministry, he lived up to his nickname in many different ways.

**He Provided for the Needy**
Luke provides this wonderful testimony of the Jerusalem church:

> And the congregation of those who believed were of one heart and soul; and not one of them claimed that anything belonging to him was his own, but all things were common property to them. And with great power the apostles were giving testimony to the resurrection of the Lord Jesus, and abundant grace was upon them all. And there was not a needy person among them, for all who were owners of land or houses would sell them and bring the proceeds of the sales and lay them at the apostles' feet, and they would be distributed to each as any had need (Acts 4:32–35).

Barnabas was one of these givers. He owned a tract of land as well, so he "sold it and brought the money and laid it at the apostles' feet" (Acts 4:37).

A Christian who supports his brethren is a boon to a church family. He doesn't do it to get noticed, but people can't help but notice and be encouraged, whether they receive his help, or simply witness his helping others.

These gifts of encouragement can be costly, such as giving away a used car, or housing and feeding a displaced family. I don't imagine Barnabas sold the very tract of land he was living on—giving freely is not the same as Communism, and people still have a primary responsibility to support their own families (1 Timothy 5:8; Ephesians 4:28). Still, it was a rich gift.

On the other hand, these gifts of encouragement don't have to cost anything. A Son of Encouragement simply can be the first to show up at worship and last to leave. He or she can volunteer for workdays and teaching, can prepare food for the bereaved, can drive to the store, or take a turn watching at a bedside. "Our people must also learn to engage in good deeds to meet pressing needs, so that they will not be unfruitful" (Titus 3:14). "But as for you, brethren, do not grow weary in doing good" (2 Thessalonians 3:13).

### He Supported the Downcast
When Luke first introduces us to Saul, he is a Jewish persecutor of Christians, a violent and hateful man scouring the territory of Israel for people to imprison (Acts 8:3). He was so successful, he decided to expand the reach of his terror to Damascus (Acts 9:1–2). On the road to Damascus, Jesus appeared to Saul personally and bodily. Three days later, Saul learned the gospel from Ananias, and became a Christian.

He proclaimed Christ in Damascus, but death threats forced him to flee. When he returned to Jerusalem, "he was trying to associate with the disciples; but they were all afraid of him, not believing that he was a disciple" (9:26). Their reluctance was understandable; the last time they saw Saul, he was presiding over the execution of their Christian brother Stephen! They refused to grant him fellowship.

Enter Barnabas:

> But Barnabas took hold of him and brought him to the apostles and described to them how he had seen the Lord on the road, and that He had talked to him, and how at Damascus he had spoken out boldly in the name of Jesus (9:27).

Only Barnabas was willing to give Paul a chance. And he did so at great risk to himself and his fellow Christians. He also put forth great effort. The word Luke chooses to describe how Barnabas "took hold of him" is the same word he uses in Acts 21:33 to describe Paul's arrest. A Son of Encouragement grabs hold when you need to be rescued and won't let go! If you've ever been in a situation where it seems like the whole world is shunning you, one person willing to be a true friend is like a ray of sunshine.

That Barnabas was willing to extend grace to Saul does not suggest that Barnabas was ignoring people's sins, receiving everyone into fellowship despite their false religion or bad behavior. He was not Son of Naiveté, or Son of Spinelessness. But he was willing to believe that Jesus changes hearts. He was willing to give people the benefit of the doubt, to forgive freely and fully, to show "mercy with cheerfulness" (Romans 12:8), to see the best in them as Christ sees.

Some weeks ago, I had a not-so-great jog. I was slow, sore, and distracted. My running app didn't say, "That was the worst run you've ever had." It said, "That was your 278th best run!" Boy, that made me feel better! Barnabas was willing to help people see the better side of things, to give thanks in all circumstances.

Later, in Acts 15:35-41, Barnabas is again the giver of second chances. Paul refused to bring Mark on an evangelistic tour, since Mark had abandoned them last time. Barnabas took Mark and went in a different direction. This was not a sad schism, for both groups did effective works in Christ. If anything, they doubled their effectiveness. And perhaps Barnabas' kindness kept Mark strong in the faith; later, Paul speaks highly of Mark (Colossians 4:10; 2 Timothy 4:11).

**He Evangelized the Lost**
One who is willing to help provide the needs of the body will also comprehend the importance of providing the needs of the soul. It should be no surprise, then, to see Barnabas broadening the circle beyond the church, to reach out to the lost. He was instrumental in evangelizing the area around

Antioch. And he was one of the very first to begin sharing the gospel with Gentiles.

> So then those who were scattered because of the persecution that occurred in connection with Stephen made their way to Phoenicia and Cyprus and Antioch, speaking the word to no one except to Jews alone. But there were some of them, men of Cyprus and Cyrene, who came to Antioch and began speaking to the Greeks also, preaching the Lord Jesus. And the hand of the Lord was with them, and a large number who believed turned to the Lord. The news about them reached the ears of the church at Jerusalem, and they sent Barnabas off to Antioch. Then when he arrived and witnessed the grace of God, he rejoiced and began to encourage them all with resolute heart to remain true to the Lord; for he was a good man, and full of the Holy Spirit and of faith. And considerable numbers were brought to the Lord. And he left for Tarsus to look for Saul; and when he had found him, he brought him to Antioch. And for an entire year they met with the church and taught considerable numbers; and the disciples were first called Christians in Antioch (Acts 11:19–26).

When the apostles in Jerusalem needed someone to teach and build up this work where Jews and Gentiles were coming together in Christ (which we know in other places was not always smooth) Barnabas was their man. He did his part reaching out, and brought in Saul to help with the work. The best encouragement we can provide is news of salvation! I can't help but wonder if it was Barnabas who brought the church into unity by saying, "I know, whether Jew or Gentile, let's just call ourselves Christians!"

**He Was in It for God's Glory, Not His Own**
In a real sense, the first missionary journey was more Barnabas' missionary journey than Paul's. It was Barnabas who went and found Paul and brought him to Antioch (Acts 11:25). It was Barnabas whose name was mentioned first by the Holy Spirit, who said, "Set apart for Me Barnabas and Saul for the work to which I have called them" (13:2). It was Barnabas' home turf of

Cyprus they went to first. The first four times their names are mentioned, Barnabas is mentioned first (Acts 12:25; 13:1–2; 13:7). Only at 13:42 does Paul take center stage. Had his role as an Apostle suddenly become clear through the miracles in Cyprus? Was his speaking more powerful and convincing?

I have no idea. But the Scripture never records that Barnabas showed a moment of jealousy or bitterness, or made any effort to take back the spotlight. Barnabas wasn't in it for his own glory, but for God's glory. A Son of Encouragement is thrilled to be eclipsed, for this means the kingdom is going to grow even more!

It is said that one day a reporter approached Leonard Bernstein, the composer and conductor of the New York Philharmonic, and asked "What is the hardest instrument in the orchestra to play?" Bernstein replied, "Second fiddle." First violin gets all the attention and all the solos, while second and third violins provide harmony. Still, their parts are exceedingly important. It's a challenge to come to every practice and put in just as much emotion and effort into their parts as the first violins do.

For every Peter, there is an Andrew who brought him to the Lord (John 1:41); for every Timothy, there is a Lois and Eunice who taught him the word (2 Timothy 1:5). Let us play our parts in the kingdom with gusto, and be excited when our efforts make it possible for others to shine the light of the gospel more brightly than we do.

# Questions for Thought

1.  What simple but generous act was Barnabas first involved in?

2.  Why was Barnabas' grabbing Paul such a courageous act of grace?

3.  What was the eventual outcome of Barnabas' willingness to extend a second chance to John Mark?

4.  Why was evangelism such a natural next step for a Son of Encouragement like Barnabas?

5.  What should our reaction be when a brother has even more results than we do in helping the lost?

# Stephen:
## *Portrait of Courage*

As THE DISCIPLES WENT THROUGH Jerusalem proclaiming Jesus' name, the Jews got increasingly upset. They questioned and briefly jailed Peter and John (Acts 4:1–22). Then, they flogged them and ordered them to be silent (5:40). Finally, their rage focused on an outspoken servant of the Lord named Stephen.

Before we see what happens, let's note that Stephen did not develop his great courage in the face of persecution overnight.

Stephen's courage began with humble service. When the church sought for servants to serve food to widows, Stephen was a man "of good reputation, full of the Spirit and of wisdom" appointed to this task (6:3).

Stephen soon grew in stature. "Stephen, full of grace and power, was performing great wonders and signs among the people" (6:8). He preached Christ publicly in the synagogues, and reasoned effectively with the most educated among them (6:9-10). Brethren who preach and teach often start small, holding the door and helping pass the communion plate!

Stephen's courage grew with study. The leaders of the synagogue "were unable to cope with the wisdom and the Spirit with which he was speaking" (6:10). Brethren who teach such powerful messages have worked to make themselves familiar with the whole Bible. Stephen's ability to speak loudly against the Jews face-to-face came from hours spent studying the Scriptures. Courage comes from moral clarity, and moral clarity comes from knowledge of God's ways and God's word.

Rather than confess the name of Jesus, the Jews in the synagogue brought Stephen before the Jewish Council. They leveled at Stephen false charges, and that's where the real drama begins.

The longest of Peter's sermons that Luke records in the book of Acts is 22 verses long (in Acts 2). The longest of Paul's sermons that Luke records is 25 verses long (in Acts 13). Paul's famous sermon on Mars Hill is just 10 verses long, and his defenses before the Jewish mobs and Councils are not much longer. But the longest sermon Luke records in the book of Acts was given by Stephen! It is 52 verses long. It must be important.

Stephen does not respond to the Jews' charges that he was speaking out against the temple and the Law (6:13)—though by the end of his sermon it is clear that he is neither anti-Moses nor anti-Temple.

In fact, Stephen's main goal does not seem to be trying to convert their hearts to Jesus as the Christ. That was more his goal in 6:9-10. At this point, the Jews' rejection of Jesus was a foregone conclusion. Stephen's goal now is to go through the whole Old Testament to explain the roots of their rejection of Jesus and to warn them of the wrath they were building up for themselves. What a courageous sermon!

Stephen says that throughout history God sent saviors to His people, but each time a large segment of His people rejected His saviors. His outline is something like this: God gave the land to the descendants of Abraham (7:2–8). Those same patriarchs became jealous and sold Joseph into Egyptian slavery (7:9–10); nevertheless God made Joseph prosper and through him saved the descendants of Abraham from extinction (7:11–16). When Israel's situation in Egypt turned sour, God sent Moses (7:17–23). Nevertheless, Israel rejected Moses and refused to follow him (7:24–37), refused to listen to the words God had given to him (7:38–43), refused to worship exclusively at the temple he built according to God's pattern (7:44) even though God is not really confined to a box on earth (7:45–50). Stephen reaches his climax:

> You men who are stiff-necked and uncircumcised in heart and ears are always resisting the Holy Spirit; you are doing just as your fathers did. Which one of the prophets did you fathers not persecute? They killed those who had previously announced the coming of the

Righteous One, whose betrayers and murderers you have now become; you who received the law as ordained by angels, and yet did not keep it (7:51–53).

These accusations infuriated the Sanhedrin. "They were cut to the quick," a phrase similar to the phrase Luke uses to describe the Jews on the day of Pentecost who were "pricked in the heart" (2:37). Unlike the Jews who on that occasion repented, the Sanhedrin lashed out in anger (7:54). A confrontation with the gospel rarely leaves one in the middle—it demands acceptance and worship, or it demands rejection and lashing out.

Stephen must have suspected what was coming next, but he did not waver for a moment. "Being full of the Holy Spirit" he was granted a vision of "Jesus standing at the right hand of God" (7:55–56), a visual confirmation of that fact which he had heretofore accepted solely on faith, that Jesus was the Christ the Son of God, and that He was not only resurrected, but had ascended to the right hand of God, serving as Lord and high priest, ruling over all things and interceding for the saints through His blood (Psalm 110:2; Ephesians 1:22–23; Hebrews 1:8). The Sanhedrin said Jesus was dead; Stephen knew Jesus was alive and reigning!

With such a confirmation of the truth of His words, and moreover, such a glimpse of the promised glory that awaited him, Stephen did not get upset. His face was bright (6:15). He was not full of dread but anticipation, saying, "Lord Jesus, receive my spirit." (7:59).

Moreover, he said, "Lord, do not hold this sin against them!" (7:60). Even at this brutal end, Stephen's goal in speaking was to glorify Jesus not himself, to preach gospel truth to all including his enemies, so that they could enjoy the same hope of salvation. May we learn to pray for our enemies and to forgive those who trespass against us (Matthew 5:43–48; 6:14–15; Luke 23:34)! Saul was part of this murderous crowd—thanks be to God that Saul did not get what justice demanded and that Stephen's prayer for forgiveness was answered through him in a mighty way. Just think of how many were converted to Jesus and gained salvation due to Stephen's courage and forbearance!

Thus, Stephen became the first Christian "martyr." This word actually means "witness." It appears 34 times in the New Testament. Though it doesn't gain the definition of one who dies for his testimony until a full century after the New Testament writing; nevertheless, death is a fate that true witnesses often met (Acts 22:20; Revelation 2:13).

Stoning is a horrible method of execution. I have read about recent examples in Muslim countries where it is sometimes still practiced, and it is not a quick or painless death. It involves blows coming from all directions, bruises, blood, broken teeth and bones, before the condemned stumbles and is finished off with heavy stones. All the while, Stephen focused on Jesus, not the injuries.

Luke testifies that he simply "fell asleep" with Jesus' name on his lips. This is a powerful point: after the resurrection of Jesus, no Bible passage speaks of the death of a Christian, but uses the euphemism, "fell asleep." Sleep is nothing to fear, it is something to embrace. It is a reminder of the victory over death provided to all who are in Christ, that those who sleep in Christ shall soon awake to glory!

Stephen's courage came from a life of study of the promises of God, and a life of service to others. May the courage of Stephen be present in the church today!

# Questions for Thought

1. When we first meet Stephen, what is his role?

2. How does Stephen's preaching in the synagogue go?

3. In his lengthy sermon before the Sanhedrin, what does he use Joseph and Moses to illustrate?

4. What impressive things happen at the very end, while Stephen is suffering execution?

5. Why does Luke use the phrase "fell asleep"?

# Eutychus:
## *Dedicated Worshiper*

On Paul's third missionary journey, he made his way back through the churches of Greece, Macedonia, and Asia Minor, with his face set toward Jerusalem.

When he arrived in Troas, he waited there for a whole week, probably so that he could be present with the disciples at a worship service on the Lord's Day.

> On the first day of the week, when we were gathered together to break bread, Paul began talking to them, intending to leave the next day, and he prolonged his message until midnight. There were many lamps in the upper room where we were gathered together (Acts 20:7–8).

Of course, this is the passage that all long-winded preachers use to berate the audience for not indulging them. But in all seriousness, the second half of Paul's third missionary journey had the flavor of a farewell tour. Paul had much to say to encourage these disciples, whom he would not see next Wednesday or next Sunday, in fact might not see for a very long time, perhaps ever again (Acts 20:25, 38; 21:5). What Paul had to say was worth hearing, and he wanted to pack as much as he possibly could into their time together. They probably asked him a lot of questions, too. Thus, he kept talking meaningfully all the way until midnight.

Suddenly the meeting was disturbed:

> There was a young man named Eutychus sitting on the window sill, sinking into a deep sleep; and as Paul kept on talking, he was overcome by sleep and fell down from the third floor and was picked up dead. But Paul went down and fell upon him, and after embrac-

ing him, he said, "Do not be troubled, for his life is in him" (Acts 20:9–10).

And of course, this is the passage that all long-winded preachers use to scold those who drift off in a pew. But I believe Eutychus gets a bad rap.

In Paul's day, many Christians were slaves. I personally like to think that perhaps Eutychus was a slave. He was probably in his late teens or early twenties: "young man," *neanias,* usually describes men from 20 to 40, but "boy" in verse 12, *paida,* suggests the early edge of this range. I don't want to assume too much that Luke doesn't reveal, but Eutychus could have worked hard all day, and was faced with the prospect of getting up the next morning and doing it all over again. Yet, Eutychus was there, assembled together with the disciples in Troas, to hear the apostle Paul's teaching rather than home relaxing or out partying. Despite his ache and exhaustion, he still managed to drag himself to worship with a smile on his face. When Paul talked until midnight, with the dim oil flames causing shapes to flicker and dance lazily on the walls, Eutychus stayed without looking at his watch and moaning. Maybe he had taken up a position on the window sill to get some cool air to help him stay alert.

But Eutychus just couldn't fight off sleep. When slumber overcame him and he slumped over, he fell three stories to the ground. The disciples rushed down and he "was picked up dead." Paul rushes down as well, and rather than lecture on the judgment coming to lousy members who can't keep their eyes open in services, Paul embraced him and comforted them with words of life.

Was Eutychus truly dead, and Paul raised him miraculously, or was Eutychus just stunned and Paul diagnosed him as just knocked out and going to be fine? I'm not sure. But in either case, the assembly wasn't finished. They went back to the upper room, broke the bread together, and continued talking with Paul all the way until dawn (Acts 20:11)!

"They took away the boy alive, and were greatly comforted" (20:12). Paul's traveling companions boarded a ship for the next town of Assos, though Paul decided to follow up his all-night marathon lesson with a nice walk (20:13–14). Perhaps like Jesus having spiritual food to eat after speaking to the woman at the well, Paul had energy to spare after such an uplifting night of worship!

Let me draw two conclusions. First, the story of Eutychus provides no comfort to those who stay awake until 4:00 AM playing video games, who then drift off during worship service. Participating in teaching and preaching is an act of worship (Acts 2:42; 1 Timothy 4:13), and nodding off during a lesson is not an insult to the preacher, but rather an insult to God. Make worship enough of a priority that you give God the best you can give, even if that means limiting your activities on Saturday night.

Second, the story of Eutychus reminds us how important worship assembly is. It is uplifting when brethren defy the world to show up at services. Some families have many responsibilities, must find ways to arrange shift work, must compromise with extracurricular activities, must wake up an hour early to get the kids breakfast and dressed. One member where I attend must work on Wednesday night, but takes his lunch break during that hour so he can attend most of the Bible study. Worship helps us learn the difference between what is merely urgent and what is truly important.

Someone told me a story of an old preacher who visited a wayward member in his home one chilly autumn evening. They sat before the fireplace, as the preacher encouraged the man to start bringing his family to services regularly. As he spoke, he used the tongs to separate the logs and coals in the fireplace. In a matter of minutes, the flames had completely died out, the coals were greying over, and the fireplace gave off little heat. He used the tongs to once again bring together the coals, and flames soon sprang up. The preacher pointed out to the member how important it is for brethren to assemble together, to keep one another on fire for the Lord.

What does assembling together provide? Hebrews 10:24–25 says,

> Let us consider how to stimulate one another to love and good
> deeds, not forsaking our own assembling together, as is the habit of
> some, but encouraging one another, and all the more as you see the
> day drawing near.

Our "assembling together" stimulates the body to love and good deeds. It
encourages the whole church. In a world that's against us, it reminds us that
there are like-minded people. When we "greet the friends by name" (3 John
15) it fills us with love and acceptance. When an elderly brother struggles to
get in the door on Sunday morning, it edifies the rest of us who see his faith.
When we take our "meals together with gladness and sincerity of heart"
(Acts 2:46) we draw closer to one another.

Worship has a special place in assembling together. Colossians 3:16–17 says,

> Let the word of Christ richly dwell within you, with all wisdom
> teaching and admonishing one another with psalms and hymns and
> spiritual songs, singing with thankfulness in your hearts to God.

When you sing *How Beautiful Heaven Must Be* it edifies not just your heart
but the heart of every other person in the room. When you sing of *The Old
Rugged Cross* you aren't just letting those scenes burst on your own mind,
but on everyone else's, too. When you sing *What a Friend We Have in Jesus*
you aren't just reminding yourself, you are convincing everyone else that it's
true. When you make a comment in class, everyone else benefits from your
insight. When you say "Amen" in prayer, the Lord hears.

Eutychus reminds me that assembling for worship should be a non-negotia-
ble priority in my life!

# Questions for Thought

1. Has your attitude toward Eutychus been negative or positive? After reading this, is it possible to see him in a different light?

2. Whatever you think of Eutychus, why do people have trouble being enthusiastic in worship?

3. Why is it important to make assemblies a priority?

4. What are some things we can do to improve our attention span and involvement in worship?

# Priscilla and Aquila:
## *A Couple for Christ*

MOST OF THE ENTRIES IN THIS SERIES on the contributions of minor characters of the New Testament have been individuals. But one of my favorite examples of Christians who stood out for their work is a married couple: Priscilla and Aquila. They demonstrate that a husband and wife, devoted to one another and devoted to God, can accomplish much for the Lord. We first meet them in Acts 18:1–4,

> After these things [Paul] left Athens and went to Corinth. And he found a Jew named Aquila, a native of Pontus, having recently come from Italy with his wife Priscilla, because Claudius had commanded all the Jews to leave Rome. He came to them, and because he was of the same trade, he stayed with them and they were working, for by trade they were tent-makers. And he was reasoning in the synagogue every Sabbath and trying to persuade Jews and Greeks.

Priscilla means "little old lady" and Aquila means "eagle." Every time the Bible mentions them they are mentioned together, with no exceptions. Luke describes them as Jews from the far northern province of Pontus, who had been living in Rome until they were exiled by the edict of Claudius. Paul met them in Corinth while proclaiming the gospel in the synagogue every Sabbath. Paul "stayed with them." Whether they became Christians before or after they met Paul is difficult to know.

Paul began working with Priscilla and Aquila because they were of the same tent-making trade. But they continued working together for the same Lord! Paul preached in Corinth for 18 months. When the persecution became intense, he departed for his home base of Antioch. Priscilla and Aquila boarded the ship with him (Acts 18:18). Paul must have had plans for them. Paul made only a brief stop in Ephesus, and left Priscilla and Aquila there (18:19) while he went on to Antioch. Clearly, Paul had a tremendous degree of confidence in their ability to establish the gospel work in Ephesus in his absence, until he could return on his third journey.

Stop and consider the commitment Priscilla and Aquila showed by moving their home and business—by choice this time—in order to serve God. I have known many who moved for a better job, a better climate, a better house, but not many who moved to help a church. This would require husband and wife to be in perfect agreement with putting God's work ahead of their own desires. What a powerful example!

Paul's trust in them was well-placed:

> A Jew named Apollos, an Alexandrian by birth, an eloquent man, came to Ephesus; and he was mighty in the Scriptures. This man had been instructed in the way of the Lord; and being fervent in spirit, he was speaking and teaching accurately the things concerning Jesus, being acquainted only with the baptism of John; and he began to speak out boldly in the synagogue. But when Priscilla and Aquila heard him, they took him aside and explained to him the way of God more accurately. And when he wanted to go across to Achaia, the brethren encouraged him and wrote to the disciples to welcome him; and when he had arrived he greatly helped those who had believed through grace, for he powerfully refuted the Jews in public, demonstrating by the Scriptures that Jesus was the Christ (Acts 18:24–28).

Imagine two tent makers from the frontier having the knowledge and courage to gently school an educated, eloquent man from Alexandria. He was "mighty in the Scriptures" but still had something to learn from the "little old lady" and her husband! Thankfully Apollos stood corrected, and went on to win many souls in Corinth.

Here's the takeaway: When a married couple is committed to God, they become an exceptionally powerful force. One of the reasons Paul says that singlehood is a great option for those with the gift of celibacy, is because "one who is married is concerned about the things of the world, how he may please his wife ... [and the wife] how she may please her husband" (1 Corinthians 7:33–34). But, what if both partners in the union are equally devoted to pleasing the Lord?

There are many things in this life that are accomplished more productively when working as a team. Most everyone can curl more weight with a two-handed barbell than the sum of each arm curling one-handed dumbbells (my very unscientific research suggests about 15-20% more). I suspect part of it is psychological, and part of it is from increased stability. Two people can accomplish a chore more than twice as fast as one person working alone. Cooperation keeps such jobs running smoothly. Companionship makes labor less of a drudgery.

When a man and woman work together as a team, there is very little they cannot accomplish, and there is very little that can come between them. This is obviously true in worldly things—they support each other's efforts; they pool their resources. But this is also true in the kingdom of God. A faithful couple helps prevent the ingress of temptations that would otherwise conquer those left alone and bored. Their mutual championing supplies a source of diligent labor for the Lord's church. When she must prepare excellent material for her upcoming kids' Bible class, he picks up the slack in chores. When he must take an evening to teach a prospective convert, she doesn't bemoan the loss of private relaxation in front of their favorite TV show. They gladly sacrifice for the privilege of growing the kingdom.

Priscilla and Aquila must have stayed in Ephesus a while, for when Paul returns and writes a letter to Corinth, he sends their greetings. He also mentions "the church that is in their house" (1 Corinthians 16:19). This reveals another example of their joint dedication. They hosted, at minimum, a weekly worship service in their home. Both husband and wife must be devoted to hospitality to view this constant intrusion as a worthwhile blessing (see 1 Peter 4:9; Romans 12:13). Think of how hard it is to convince a family to host a single pot luck these days. Now, imagine hosting the whole congregation, every Sunday! There would be no staying in bed on a cold

Sunday, no refusing to get ready because of aches or the sniffles. Priscilla and Aquila's care for the brethren puts most of us to shame. They arranged every aspect of their lives, from business to leisure to travel, according to the priorities of the kingdom.

This was their pattern everywhere they lived. Some months later, when Paul wrote Romans, Priscilla and Aquila had moved back to Rome. Paul mentions them and says,

> Greet Prisca and Aquila, my fellow workers in Christ Jesus, who for my life risked their own necks, to whom not only do I give thanks, but also all the churches of the Gentiles; also greet the church that is in their house (Romans 16:3–5).

What an enthusiastic couple! Their work involved not only hospitality and evangelism, but danger. There were perhaps many instances in which their property and safety were threatened. All the Gentiles who traced their eternal salvation back to their goodness and faithfulness made the physical risks worthwhile. Would that modern couples dared to be so kind and so bold!

Priscilla and Aquila were in it for life. Around twenty years later, they are two of the last people Paul affectionately mentions as he closes his final letter (2 Timothy 4:19), probably from a cold cell. There they are, still busy, still beloved, decades after their first meeting in Corinth.

Married Christians, be a team for Christ! Help one another get to worship. Make it easy for one another to serve the brethren in your respective ways, and also together. Make it possible for one another to reach out to unbelievers. Agree to arrange your careers and your child-rearing around the common goal of being a force for good in your congregation. Leave a legacy of faith to the next generation, to your children and even your grandchildren. Get excited together about structuring your finances, your investments, and your giving around the Lord's priorities. Cooperate to make your travels and your hobbies subordinate to opportunities to glorify the Lord.

One more thing: I hope this doesn't offend anyone terribly, but I have for the umpteenth time met an elder of the Lord's church who is looking forward to retirement. He has spent many years as a figurehead, but has been forced to give his greatest time and efforts to his secular job. Sure, he has attended elders' meetings and made some decisions about the building fund, but it's hard to squeeze in real shepherding when one must punch a clock. Now that he is ready to leave his job, he is looking forward to moving into a cabin in the mountains. Say it ain't so! When the church's need is the most dire, when he finally has the opportunity to exercise the kind of leadership that God has wanted him to exercise all along, to truly get involved in the lives of the flock, he's going to take a seat in a rocking chair on the porch in the comfortable hills? We need our shepherds to decide to *increase* their involvement in their congregations at retirement. In fact, I dare say the church needs elders who are willing to quit their jobs and devote 10 hours a week or more to shepherding the flock. This kind of diligent shepherding would be the sort of thing an Aquila could excel at with the help and love of a partner like Priscilla.

# Questions for Thought

1. What was the ethnic and geographical background of Priscilla and Aquila?

2. What is one thing they did better together as a team than they could have done as singles?

3. Another?

4. Why was their correction of Apollos so remarkable?

5. What is the key to making a marriage an asset for the kingdom of Christ?

# Tabitha:
## *Abounding in Charity*

Luke records in Acts 9:36–42,

> Now in Joppa there was a disciple named Tabitha (which translated in Greek is called Dorcas); this woman was abounding with deeds of kindness and charity which she continually did. And it happened at that time that she fell sick and died; and when they had washed her body, they laid it in an upper room. Since Lydda was near Joppa, the disciples, having heard that Peter was there, sent two men to him, imploring him, "Do not delay in coming to us." So Peter arose and went with them. When he arrived, they brought him into the upper room; and all the widows stood beside him, weeping and showing all the tunics and garments that Dorcas used to make while she was with them. But Peter sent them all out and knelt down and prayed, and turning to the body, he said, "Tabitha, arise." And she opened her eyes and when she saw Peter, she sat up. And he gave her his hand and raised her up; and calling the saints and widows, he presented her alive. It became known all over Joppa, and many believed in the Lord. And Peter stayed many days in Joppa with a tanner named Simon.

Tabitha in Hebrew, like Dorcas in Greek, refers to an animal like a doe or antelope, an Eastern symbol of graceful beauty. Who knows what Tabitha looked like to earn the appellation; but in Christ, her true beauty shone forth through "the hidden person" of her compassionate heart (1 Peter 3:4; 1 Timothy 2:10), as she provided handmade articles of clothing for the widows of the church in Lydda.

From time to time, a sister in Christ will do something sweet, like knit booties for new babies in the congregation. My family still uses the potholders handmade for us by a dear elderly sister many years ago. It's likely that

Tabitha's contribution was more than just thoughtful trinkets. In the ancient world, making garments was a very time-consuming task. "Tunics," *chitonas*, refer to the clothes worn against the body, and "garments," *himatia*, refer to the outer coverings. These were not cute outfits for babies, but were essentials of life for the poor, perhaps not only the difference between comfort and misery, but the difference between life and death (Deuteronomy 24:12; 2 Timothy 4:13).

Tabitha may not have had the financial means of Barnabas (Acts 4:36–37), but she used her time and energy to become "rich in good works" (1 Timothy 6:18). The word "abounding in" (*pleres*) literally means "full of" or "completely occupied with." Luke uses this word in various contexts to describe both positive things, like being full of grace and faith (Acts 6:5–8), or negative things like being full of deceit (Acts 13:10), rage (Acts 19:28), or disease (Luke 5:12). Luke meant it in a thoroughly positive way. When one thought of Tabitha, one couldn't help but think of her good works!
May our family in Christ in every town be just as abounding in kind deeds. God doesn't want us to enable mooching, but He does want us to rush in to assist with legitimate needs.

> We hear that some among you are leading an undisciplined life, doing no work at all, but acting like busybodies. Now such persons we command and exhort in the Lord Jesus Christ to work in quiet fashion and eat their own bread. But as for you, brethren, do not grow weary of doing good (2 Thessalonians 3:11–13).

Paul repeats his call for doing good works many places. "I want women to adorn themselves … by means of good works, as is proper for women making a claim to godliness" (1 Timothy 2:9–10). "Urge the young men to be sensible; in all things show yourself to be an example of good deeds, with purity in doctrine" (Titus 2:6–7).

> Let us not lose heart in doing good, for in due time we will reap if we do not grow weary. So then, while we have opportunity, let us do

good to all people, and especially to those who are of the household of faith" (Galatians 6:9–10).

"Pure and undefiled religion" includes not just running through the motions of religiosity, but having a heart for the hurting, alleviating the suffering of orphans and widows (James 1:27). There is love in preparing a meal for a funeral, visiting a sick person in the hospital to read and pray or just while away some minutes in pleasant conversation, offering a ride to the grocery store for shut-ins, sending a thoughtful card or gift, doing yard work and household chores for the disabled. "Our people must also learn to engage in good deeds to meet pressing needs, so that they will not be unfruitful" (Titus 3:14).

Let us never forget that our eternal judgment will be based, at least in part, on the compassion we showed.

> Then the King will say to those on His right, "Come, you who are blessed of My Father, inherit the kingdom prepared for you from the foundation of the world. For I was hungry, and you gave Me something to eat; I was thirsty, and you gave Me something to drink; I was a stranger, and you invited Me in; naked, and you clothed Me; I was sick, and you visited Me; I was in prison, and you came to Me."
> Then the righteous will answer Him, "Lord, when did we see You hungry, and feed you, or thirsty, and give You something to drink? And when did we see You a stranger, and invite You in, or naked, and clothe You? When did we see You sick, or in prison, and come to You?"
> The King will answer and say to them, "Truly I say to you, to the extent that you did it to one of these brothers of Mine, even the least of them, you did it to Me" (Matthew 25:34–40).

Those on the King's left were lost, in part, because of their refusal to act compassionately toward the hungry, the sick, the prisoner, and the stranger. When I was in school, from time to time the professor would say, "This will probably be on the test." Suddenly, one hundred drooping eyes snapped open, and fifty pencils began scratching, as every student took the professor very seriously and worked feverishly to be sure they copied the chalkboard notes thoroughly. Sure enough, that diagram or that chart would be on the test, sometimes verbatim.

Well, there are a number of things God tells us in the Bible are going to be on the test, that is, are going to be part of the basis of judgment. They include how we behave (John 5:28–29), how we judge others (Matthew 6:14–15), how we speak (Matthew 12:36–37), how we handle sin (Galatians 5:19–21), and how we lead those entrusted to our care (Hebrews 13:17). According to Jesus, how we respond to others in need will also be on the test!

One of the highest complements we find in Scripture is Jesus praising the lowly woman who anointed His body with perfume, saying, "She has done what she could" (Mark 14:8). May the same be said of each of us!

Suddenly, the significance of Tabitha's humble work was brought to the forefront by her passing. Those she had helped now held vigil over the body, wearing the garments she had made for them.

What brought Peter into the picture? Lydda and Joppa lie on the road from Azotus to Caesarea, and thus had likely been evangelized by Philip (Acts 8:40). Perhaps Peter thought it wise to make a tour of those cities, to strengthen the new disciples. Peter had come about thirty miles from Jerusalem to the area of Lydda already (9:32). When the saints begged him to come to Joppa on the coast, it was only another ten miles or so.

In Lydda, Peter had healed a man who had been paralyzed for eight years, and this remarkable miracle caused many to turn to the Lord (9:33–35). Did the saints in Joppa call on Peter expecting a miracle, even for him to raise Tabitha? Perhaps, though no apostle raises the dead anywhere else in Acts, unless we count Eutychus (Acts 20:10). I tend to think they just wanted his encouragement at this time of great distress. Perhaps his haste is explained because the burial would happen soon. Luke just doesn't say.

In any case, such tragedies often challenge our faith. If someone in Joppa had to die, why not some less-dedicated person, some high-maintenance fringe believer who rarely makes it to services? In fact, we might wonder why, if God was going to raise one Christian somewhere in Palestine, He chose to raise Tabitha in this far-flung church rather than Stephen in Jerusalem. Surely his good works outstripped hers!

We must confess ignorance, while professing faith. God doesn't often use our scale of value. In fact, maybe one lesson is that Tabitha's contributions were in God's sight equal to Stephen's. In any case, inexplicable disasters can be used by a gracious and omnipotent God to bring about good ends. Perhaps Tabitha was ready to stand before God, and her passing could bring others closer to God. In any case, the great miracle Peter performed made many people turn to the Lord. And I'm certain that whatever rhyme or reason we seek, Tabitha would be happy to bring glory to Christ, whether in death or in life. Let us strive for the same mindset.

# Questions for Thought

1.  Is there a Tabitha or two in your congregation? What's one kind deed that person has done?

2.  How do these acts of goodness grow beyond supplying a little food or a little warmth?

3.  If someone asked you, "Why did God allow Tabitha to die?" how would you respond to strengthen their faith?

4.  In what way will our good works affect our eternity?

5.  What is one deed *you* can do in the mold of Tabitha?

# Epaphroditus:
## *Fellow Worker in Christ*

WHEN WE THINK OF PAUL'S TRAVELING companions, we think first of Timothy and Titus. But there were many others who also suffered hardship, took risks, taught frequently, and worked diligently to spread the gospel. In the middle of the Philippian letter, Paul says,

> But I thought it necessary to send to you Epaphroditus, my brother and fellow worker and fellow soldier, who is also your messenger and minister to my need; because he was longing for you all and was distressed because you heard that he was sick. For indeed he was sick to the point of death, but God had mercy on him, and not on him only but also on me, so that I would not have sorrow upon sorrow. Therefore, I have sent him all the more eagerly so that when you see him again you may rejoice and I may be less concerned about you. Receive him then in the Lord with all joy, and hold men like him in high regard; because he came close to death for the work of Christ, risking his life to complete what was deficient in your service to me (Philippians 2:25–30).

English owes a lot to Greek, from hypodermic needles to hyperbaric chambers, from pseudonyms to claustrophobia, from amethysts to petroglyphs, from televisions and telescopes. Even little words like phone and zoo are based on Greek. For the most part, the thorny issues of translating Greek manuscripts into English should be left to the experts. But now and then, a Greek Bible dictionary can, when handled carefully, uncover some interesting truths.

One of the most common Greek roots is the prefix *syn-*. You can see this in English words like synonym and synagogue and synchrony and syllogism and sympathy and symphony and even system (in Greek, *syn-* changes to *sym-*, *syl-*, *sys-*, *syg-*, or *sy-*, before certain letters). Any time the prefix *syn-* attaches to a word, it introduces the idea of togetherness and cooperation, of doing something *with* someone else.

The Apostle Paul used a lot of words with the prefix *syn-*. In fact, he was so fond of *syn-* that he stuck it on the front of many words to coin new words, some of which have yet to be found elsewhere in the Greek language. That is, Paul took common ideas and created a new vocabulary to describe the togetherness of Christians and their efforts. Ralph Earle figures that there are over 175 compound words in the Greek New Testament with the prefix *syn-*, many of which are found nowhere else in the world except in Paul's writings (*Word Meanings in the New Testament*, p. 303).

These aren't always readily apparent. For example, Romans 8:16–17 has four *syns* in one sentence:

> The Spirit Himself **testifies with** our spirit that we are children of God, and if children, heirs also, heirs of God and **fellow heirs with** Christ, if indeed we **suffer with** Him so that we may also be **glorified with** Him.

The words are: *symmartuo,* from *martureo,* "to bear witness, to testify"; *synkleronomos,* from *kleronomos,* "an heir"; *sympascho,* from *pascho,* "to suffer"; and *syndoxazo,* from *doxazo* "to esteem as glorious." A Greek reader, seeing this repetition, would certainly be struck by how totally his fate is bound up with Christ. By this intense language Paul points out that we aren't just lapping up the scraps, but rather we are *fellow* heirs of the very same inheritance and glory that Christ Himself possesses. Whatever Christ has experienced we can expect; whatever belongs to Christ belongs to us. If we join together with Jesus Christ in suffering, if we become fellow sufferers by taking up our crosses daily, then we shall be fellow partakers in His glory.

One more example is Ephesians 2:4–6,

> But God, being rich in mercy, because of His great love with which He loved us, even when we were dead in our transgressions, **made**

*us alive together with* Christ (by grace you have been saved) and *raised us up with Him,* and *seated us with Him* in the heavenly places in Christ Jesus.

The end of this sentence (without the parenthesis) is elegantly simple, in Greek: *"synezoopoisen to Christo … kai synegeiren kai synekathisen."*

I could go on pointing out these examples all over the New Testament, but let's return to Ephaphroditus in Philippians 2:25 (whose name, by the way, derives from the Greek deity Aphrodite). Paul calls him not only a brother, but a "fellow worker," *synergon,* and "fellow soldier," *systratioten.* That is, Paul doesn't think of Epaphroditus as an assistant or a go-fer. But rather as two men so devoted to Jesus they were linked together in a common bond and working toward a common end. Their efforts were intertwined and codependent.

In the same way, Paul often recognized the coworkers he had throughout his travels, as he bore the burden of spreading the gospel. He calls Epaphras *synaikmalotos,* that is, "fellow prisoner" (Philemon 23). He calls Tychicus *syndoulos,* "fellow bond-servant," from the common word *doulos,* "slave" (Colossians 4:7). He calls Titus *synekdemos,* "traveling companion," even though most translations change the noun to a verb for the sake of clarity (2 Corinthians 8:19). Paul calls a host of people, including Prisca and Aquila in Romans 16:3, *synergos,* "fellow workers." By using *syn-,* Paul praised the worth of their contributions, and at the same time lowered himself to the level of every other humble Christian.

But it's not just those Paul names in the New Testament. Furthermore, as Christians, we are all *sympolites,* fellow members of the same heavenly nation (Ephesians 2:19). We are all *synkleronos kai syssoma kai symmetoxa,* that is, "fellow heirs, and fellow members of the body, and fellow partakers of the promise in Christ Jesus through the gospel" (Ephesians 3:6). Again, the repetition would have instantly struck Greek readers.

Members of the church are not just individuals in a social club, but are comrades merged together in a common purpose. We are not people who happen to come to the same place on Sunday morning, like people who happen to come to the same restaurant at the same time every weekend. Paul says in Ephesians 2:19–22,

> So then you … are of God's household, having been built on the foundation of the apostles and prophets, Christ Jesus Himself being the corner stone, in whom the whole building, *being fitted together*, is growing into a holy temple in the Lord, in whom you also *are being built together* into a dwelling of God in the Spirit.

Paul expresses the idea of being mortared together with two lengthy words, *synarmologeomai* and *synoikodomeo*. When Paul sticks *syn-* on the front of the words *harmos*, "a joint," and *oikos*, "a house," he evokes the image of thick walls emerging from the stones, and the tongues of boards being driven snugly into the adjoining grooves. We may have our individual places in God's temple, but we are an interdependent structure. We are built up together, or we collapse together.

Need more? Our hearts are to be "knit together in love", *symbibazo* (Colossians 2:2). Paul demands that we be *symmimetes*, not just an "imitator," but a fellow imitator (Philippians 3:17). In Hebrews 10:34 we are to show sympathy, *sympatheo*. In Romans 1:11–12 Paul was looking forward to seeing the brethren so he could both give and receive encouragement, *symparakaleo*. Later in Romans 15:32 he wanted to find "refreshing rest in your company," a fitting way to translate the word *synanapauomai*. In Romans 15:30 he hoped they would "strive together with me," *synagonizomai*. In Philippians 1:27 he uses a similar term *synathleo*. In Philippians 2:18 Paul invites the brethren to "share your joy with me," *synchairo*, from *chairo*, "to rejoice." In Philippians 4:14 he commends them for "sharing with me in my affliction" *synkoinoneo*, an intense form of the word for "fellowship." As Christians reading the same Bible we are to be *synpsuchos*, "of the same mind" (Philippians 2:2), and we jointly help, *synypourgeo*, with our prayers, even when we are distant (2 Corinthians 1:11).

Let us all see the responsibilities of togetherness with Christ and togetherness with His church!

Is it any wonder then, why the thought of losing Epaphroditus to sickness deeply upset Paul? He was as dependent on Epaphroditus' companionship as a vine is to a trellis. But if Paul knew his own peace of mind depended on Epaphroditus, more so the Philippians' peace of mind. Thus, he decided to deprive himself of Epaphroditus' help, and send him back home, where he could be an encouragement to the whole church.

Such a man who had "risked his life"—whether by taxing his poor health, or by an unmentioned example of persecution—was surely a huge help to any congregation.

Note that the phrase "what was lacking on your part" doesn't indicate an insult against the Philippians as it may first seem. The Philippians were simply unable to help (compare 1 Corinthians 16:18 and especially Colossians 1:24). Epaphroditus served as their messenger (Philippians 4:18).

With all this in mind, may God send us many more like Ephaphroditus, Christians whose lives are intertwined with ours as with Christ's. Such men are a great example, and we should "hold in high regard" their service.

# Questions for Thought

1. What does the Greek root *syn-* do to any word it is attached to?

2. No Christian can be as effective alone as he can with supporters and fellow workers. How did Epaphroditus help Paul?

3. How did Epaphroditus help the Philippian church?

4. How can we help one another?

5. How might we do as Paul says, to "hold men like him in high regard"?

# Titus:
## *Preacher in the Hard Places*

THOUGH TITUS IS NOT MENTIONED by name in the book of Acts, we can safely assume he was involved in many of Paul's journeys, from a very early time.

In Galatians 2:1–2 Paul says, "I went up to Jerusalem with Barnabas, taking Titus along also. It was because of a revelation that I went up." If this refers to the visit to Jerusalem recorded in Acts 11:30 and 12:25 (which, according to Acts 11:28, was indeed prompted by a revelation), then Titus would have been Paul's traveling companion six or seven years before Timothy came on the scene.

What was the nature of the relationship between Paul and Titus? Paul calls Titus "a true child in a common faith" (Titus 1:4). Now, Paul is not suggesting that Titus owes his salvation to Paul, nor that he must approach God through the intermediary of Paul. Every Christian's mediator is Jesus alone (1 Timothy 2:5). For this reason, we are careful not to address other Christians as "Father" or "Reverend" in the sense of a spiritual hierarchy (Matthew 23:8–10). If in some way Paul introduced Titus to the gospel, it is still as equal participants in a "common faith," not as an Amway recruiter assembling a pyramid of underlings. Paul calls Titus a "true child" because they shared an affectionate relationship like a father and son. Titus also heeded Paul's directions in ministry.

Let me put it this way: I can't imagine Titus bowing and kissing Paul's ring and calling him Holy Father; but I can imagine Titus submitting to Paul's request to spread the gospel to a particular town. Paul said, "I urged Titus to go" (2 Corinthians 12:18). He said this to others, too: "Tychicus I have sent to Ephesus" (2 Timothy 4:12). Even in giving instructions, though, I see cooperation and freedom. These ministers deferred to Paul's plans; though some did not always (Acts 13:13; 2 Timothy 4:10). Paul didn't boss

Titus around. Paul calls Titus "my partner and fellow worker among you" (2 Corinthians 8:23). He praised Titus' work for God,

> Thanks be to God who puts the same earnestness on your behalf in the heart of Titus. For he not only accepted our appeal, but being himself very earnest, he has gone to you of his own accord" (2 Corinthians 8:16–17).

It's quite impossible to recreate a full map or timeline of Titus' travels. But it is clear that Paul entrusted Titus with the work of spreading the gospel in places Paul could not be. In fact, if any pattern emerges, it is that Titus seems to pop up with the most challenging assignments.

Corinth was a tough place. In 1 Corinthians, Paul admonishes the brethren for everything from sowing division to defrauding one another to suing one another to idolatry to fornication to making chaos out of worship. Many of them had come out of a sinful lifestyle, and were lagging in their maturity in Christ. Not what we'd call a plum assignment. Not the kind of congregation that most preachers would express a desire to work with.

Though there are a couple of other ways to reconstruct the data, it would seem that after sending 1 Corinthians, Paul learned of even more trouble. From Ephesus, he wrote them another very harsh letter, refusing to come right away as he had intended. Instead, he sent Titus in a clockwise direction to Corinth, ahead of his own visit, while he continued in a counterclockwise direction preaching in the cities of Macedonia. He expected they would run into each other in Troas, where Paul could get a report of the Corinthians' disposition and reaction to his letter. But when Titus didn't show up (2 Corinthians 2:13) Paul could not rest and hastened onward. When he finally found Titus, he was overjoyed to discover that most of the Corinthians had responded favorably to his letter (7:6–7) and had in fact treated Titus kindly (7:13–16).

This must have been quite a nerve-wracking assignment for Titus, to be Paul's rod of admonition, without the presence of the apostle himself.

But think of the false teaching and immorality that would have spread unchecked throughout the congregation without a diligent preacher like Titus ready to enter the fray.

Titus also was central to arranging and collecting the offering of Gentile churches for suffering brethren in Judea (2 Corinthians 8:6). Like all requests for money, this must have been a delicate yet bold work. He proved himself capable and trustworthy (2 Corinthians 8:21; 12:18).

When we see Titus again, about ten years later, Paul had dispatched him to another difficult assignment, to remain on the island of Crete, "that you would set in order what remains and appoint elders in every city as I directed you" (Titus 1:5). Titus was up against rebels, "empty talkers and deceivers, especially those of the circumcision, who must be silenced because they are upsetting whole families, teaching things they should not teach" (1:10–11). Paul suggested that Cretans have a reputation as "liars, evil beasts, and lazy gluttons" (1:12–13) and thus needed to be severely reproved. Evidently, Titus was the right man to do the reproving.

Too often, preachers look for a comfortable assignment, an encouraging audience, a big and healthy congregation. This can be nice at certain points in life, especially when first starting out, or when raising children. But, let our preachers stop thinking about what's easy and palatable for them, and start thinking about what's best for the Lord and for the kingdom. Titus never left a church because it wasn't what he expected a good congregation to be. He *went* to such churches, and worked diligently to help them *become* what a good congregation should be. Too often the best preachers seek out congregations where most everything is already chugging along on all eight cylinders, where a board of loving and godly elders are already doing a great job leading and teaching.

The biggest needs are elsewhere, with struggling churches in small towns or cities outside the Bible belt. From time to time, when I take vacations or hiking trips, I will make a point to worship with whatever congregation is nearby. I am upset to admit it, but in almost every case I have found congregations running on fumes, who haven't filled the baptistery in years, were almost every member is over the age of 60, where the elders (if there are elders) are content to keep the lights on while they manage the decline. Where the members congratulate themselves for "standing for the truth" when there hasn't been an effort to reach out with the truth in decades. There's more to being a sound church than avoiding evil. The Jerusalem church evangelized daily! Something must be done in these places to reinvigorate the work, or there will be no church there in twenty years. Our children will find a landscape with fewer congregations to attend.

Now I know that people plant and water the seed and God gives the increase, and I am willing to accept that in some places there is no increase to be given. But I tend to think it has more to do with our planting and watering. There's a lot of blame to go around, but I place a lot of the blame on preachers who find it easy to keep a congregation happy by downloading a sermon outline or two during the week, and doing the public speaking, but who haven't thought about what makes God happy. May God send us preachers who think more like first responders, running toward the flames and the sirens, rather than away.

If 2 Corinthians is our main source for what is said *about* Titus, the letter that bears his name is our source for what is said *to* Titus. As Titus was a faithful assistant to Paul in his role as apostle to the Gentiles, modern evangelists can be faithful to Jesus Christ by following these inspired directions.

A faithful evangelist seeking to glorify Christ must "speak the things which are fitting for sound doctrine" (Titus 2:1). For Titus this included: to present the message of the gospel to men and women, young and old alike (2:2–6), to steer clear of myths and controversy (1:14–16; 3:9), to prove to be an example to all (2:7–8), to lift people's minds from the world into heavenly hope (2:9–14), to instruct them to be submissive and obedient (2:9–10; 3:1–3), to warn and even reject factious men (3:9–11), and to convince them to be involved in fruitful good deeds (3:1–8, 14). Titus kept it up until the arrival of Artemas and Tychicus, when he joined Paul in Nicopolis for the winter (3:12).

An evangelist needn't bother with speculation, and shouldn't stick his nose where it doesn't belong, but when it comes to the truth, he should "speak confidently" (3:8). "These things speak and exhort and reprove with all authority. Let no one disregard you" (2:15).

# Questions for Thought

How do you explain the seeming contradiction between Matthew 23:8-10 and Titus 1:4?

What was true of Titus' assignments at Corinth and on Crete?

What would be required for someone to prepare himself to leave a strong, encouraging congregation and work with a small, weak congregation?

What is one thing Paul told Titus to do as an effective evangelist in Crete?

What can you do?

# Timothy:
## *Busy Soldier for Christ*

WHILE SOME OF THE "MINOR CHARACTERS" we have studied may appear in just a passage or two, Timothy is mentioned throughout Acts and Paul's epistles. It almost feels inaccurate to call him a "minor" character.

There is so much to learn from Timothy's labors, one doesn't know where to start. Let's focus on one particular metaphor Paul uses to spur Timothy to faithfulness and dedication.

> Suffer hardship with me, as a good soldier of Christ Jesus. No soldier in active service entangles himself in the affairs of everyday life, so that he may please the one who enlisted him as a soldier (2 Timothy 2:3–4).

In this context, the "affairs of everyday life" aren't necessarily sinful things, but the concerns of the world that would distract Timothy from his special calling as an evangelist. Soldiers make special sacrifices to serve, and so should evangelists. Now, *every* Christian is a priest and a minister and teacher, but some devote themselves to preaching "full time." Timothy rose to the challenge of being a soldier for Christ throughout his life, giving little thought to his personal comforts, and overcoming a number of obstacles, for the privilege of preaching the word.

We first meet him in Acts 16:1–3, on Paul's second missionary journey.

> Paul came also to Derbe and to Lystra. And a disciple was there, named Timothy, the son of a Jewish woman who was a believer, but his father was a Greek, and he was well spoken of by the brethren who were in Lystra and Iconium. Paul wanted this man to go with him; and he took him and circumcised him because of the Jews who were in those parts, for they all knew that his father was a Greek.

Right away, Timothy proves his willingness to endure hardship for the sake of the gospel, submitting to circumcision. Now, in this case, circumcision had nothing to do with salvation; in fact, being circumcised in order to be saved separates one from Christ (Galatians 5:2–4)! For this reason, Paul had refused to allow Titus to be circumcised (Galatians 2:1–10). But Paul circumcised Timothy so that he would not be a stumbling block to the Jews they would encounter together, so that he would be able to speak to them in the synagogue. As Paul would say in a different place, "For though I am free from all men, I have made myself a slave to all so that I may win more" (1 Corinthians 9:19–23). As a side note, we here learn that the purpose of an action is sometimes as important as the action itself in determining its lawfulness.

Timothy must have been quite a young man, since Paul mentions Timothy's "youthfulness" around 15 years later (1 Timothy 4:12)—I've seen suggestions that range from 15 to 25. Soon, the second missionary journey proved to be broader in scope than Paul envisioned. The Spirit would not allow Paul to spend much time in "those parts" of Asia Minor, and instead called Paul to cross the sea and evangelize Europe. Timothy doesn't seem to have hesitated to follow when the field of labor got farther and farther from home.

Though Timothy's name is not mentioned for a while, we assume he was along for all the experiences, good and bad. He soon proved his worth. In Berea, persecution was so intense that Paul was escorted out of the city, but he left Timothy and Silas to strengthen the new church there (Acts 17:14–15), and then catch up when possible. It seems that Paul later redirected Timothy to nearby Thessalonica.

> We thought it best to be left behind at Athens alone, and we sent Timothy, our brother and God's fellow worker in the gospel of Christ, to strengthen and encourage you as to your faith, so that no one would be disturbed by these afflictions (1 Thessalonians 3:1–3).

Timothy soon left Thessalonica, "and brought us good news of your faith and love" (3:6) when he caught up to Paul in Corinth. And that allows us to rejoin the story in Acts 18:5,

> But when Silas and Timothy came down from Macedonia, Paul began devoting himself completely to the word, solemnly testifying to the Jews that Jesus was the Christ.

We assume that Timothy brought with him a gift of financial support, from the churches of Macedonia (Philippians 4:18), allowing Paul to evangelize full-time.

On the third journey, Paul sent Timothy to Corinth (1 Corinthians 4:17; 16:10) and later to Macedonia with Erastus (Acts 19:22). Later, he traveled with Paul on his fateful trip to Jerusalem (Acts 20:4). He was with Paul during his Roman imprisonment (Romans 16:21), and he was a cosigner of many of Paul's letters, including the ones written from prison (Philippians 1:1; Colossians 1:1; Philemon 1). Certainly, he experienced his own imprisonments too (Hebrews 13:23).

Knowing full well that Acts and the epistles don't provide a complete picture of Timothy's travels, we come away impressed with his schedule. We can only imagine that he was constantly hustling and bustling from one church to the next, bringing joy and good news and truth and rebuke in Paul's stead. He was a busy and dedicated evangelist, a soldier of Jesus, using the sword of the Spirit to spread the good news of the kingdom of God. Paul demanded a lot of him, and he rose to the challenge. He let no obstacle stand in his way.

What did soldiering for Christ mean for Timothy? From an early age, Timothy gave up whatever personal ambition and desire he may have had, to completely devote himself to the work of spreading the gospel. When his peers were having fun, he was studying to show himself approved as a workman. When his peers were building wealth, he was building churches. When his peers were focused on the "affairs of everyday life," Timothy was focused on guarding and sharing the treasure of the faith which had been entrusted to him (1 Timothy 6:20; 2 Timothy 1:14).

Soldiering for Christ also meant something else to Timothy. He let nothing deter him from full service. People are capable of mighty things for the Lord, no matter the limitations others may attempt to impose, or they may impose on themselves. I have noticed some things that could have become an excuse for Timothy. Now, we shouldn't assume too much—just because Paul encourages Timothy in a certain area doesn't necessarily mean he had been failing in that area. Nevertheless, I think we can safely identify three potential obstacles. First, some must have scoffed at Timothy's youthfulness; he did not allow this to dissuade him from preaching (1 Timothy 4:12). On the other hand, I suspect some in Lystra and Iconium, who spoke so well of Timothy to Paul, may have wished to keep his talents and energy all to themselves! Second, some must have turned up their noses at his half-Gentile ancestry; Timothy did what he could to make that less of an issue to his prospective listeners (Acts 16:3). Third, I suspect Timothy was naturally a little shy and timid, for Paul reminds him that the Christian spirit is not one of timidity, but one of "power and love and discipline" (2 Timothy 1:7), and repeatedly reminds him of the inevitability of persecution. Paul expected much of this young man, and Timothy rose to the challenge. Soldiers of Christ do not rely on their own strength, but the strength of the Lord.

If Acts shows us that Timothy was a busy evangelist, the two letters that bear his name show us *how* to be a busy evangelist. I have known preachers who spent the first few minutes in the office every Monday morning rereading 1 and 2 Timothy—not a bad idea for one determined to evangelize effectively.

While there is a lot of overlap in the two letters, Paul's emphasis in 1 Timothy is mostly on what to teach the members of the church, while 2 Timothy on how to conduct himself. This is fitting, since 2 Timothy is widely regarded as Paul's last letter to Timothy, and in fact the last of Paul's letters in the canon, an effort to pass the torch and prepare the faithful evangelist to carry on in his absence.

Because there is so much here, allow me to try to boil it down to two bulleted lists. In terms of his instruction, Paul charged Timothy with teaching members of the body of Christ "how one ought to conduct himself in the household of God" (3:15). This included:

- opposing men who taught strange doctrines (1 Timothy 1:3–20; 4:1–5; 6:3–6; 6:20–21)
- organizing worship (2:1–8; 4:13)
- organizing the care of widows (5:3–16)
- giving instruction on women (2:9–15)
- giving instruction on slaves and slave owners (6:1–2)
- giving instruction on the rich (6:6–10; 17–19)
- appointing elders and deacons (3:1–13; 5:17–22)
- training the next group of preachers (2 Timothy 2:2).

Though experience helps, obviously a preacher's ability to teach comes more from his knowledge of the truth than having walked in others' shoes—Timothy had never been a woman, a slave owner, a widow, an elder, or a rich man. Let today's evangelists strive to know the Bible thoroughly, and then teach it boldly!

In terms of his own life, Paul encouraged Timothy:

- to "fight the good fight, keeping faith and a good conscience" (1 Timothy 1:18–19)
- to get his nourishment from "sound doctrine" (4:6)
- to discipline himself for godliness (4:7; 16)
- to be so absorbed in his duties that others notice growth (4:15)
- to avoid partiality (5:21)
- to flee from the love of money (6:10–11)
- to live out his good confession of Jesus (6:12–16)
- to guard the gospel that has been entrusted to him (1:18, 6:20)
- to "kindle afresh the gift of God" (2 Timothy 1:6–7)
- to steel his resolve in the face of persecution (2 Timothy 1:8–12; 2:3; 2:8–13; 3:10–13)

- to "retain the standard of sound words" (2 Timothy 1:13) and be "accurately handling the word of truth" (2:15; 3:14–17) while at the same time remaining aloof from "wrangling about words" (2:14), "worldly and empty chatter" (2:16), and "foolish and ignorant speculation" (2:23). This is such an important distinction between what is worth preaching about and what is not. Preachers must remember that "the goal of our instruction is love from a pure heart, and a good conscience, and a sincere faith" (1 Timothy 1:5) and if our efforts don't foster one of those things, the lesson is probably more suited for a political rally than for the pulpit.
- to flee youthful lusts and instead pursue "righteousness, faith, love and peace" (2:22)
- to patiently absorb wrongs and correct gently, understanding that Satan is the real enemy not misguided brethren (2:24–26)
- to prepare himself to handle bad actors (3:1–9)
- again, and above all, to "preach the word … in season and out of season" (4:2–3).

With an image of Paul's own execution by sword sharp in his mind, Paul sums up: "be sober in all things, endure hardship, do the work of an evangelist, fulfill your ministry" (2 Timothy 4:5).

Paul leaned on Timothy and his fellow workers a lot. One of Paul's highest compliments for any of his fellow workers is for Timothy, in the middle of the Philippian letter:

> But I hope in the Lord Jesus to send Timothy to you shortly, so that I also may be encouraged when I learn of your condition. For I have no one else of kindred spirit who will genuinely be concerned for your welfare. For they all seek after their own interests, not those of Christ Jesus. But you know of his proven worth, that he served with me in the furtherance of the gospel like a child serving his father (Philippians 2:19–22).

May we all, whether called as evangelists or any other role in the Lord's body, to be "a kindred spirit" to Paul, putting the edification of the body of Christ and the spread of the gospel above all other things.

## Questions for Thought

1. In what sense was Timothy a soldier?

2. How was Timothy to overcome the concerns of those who scoffed at his youthfulness?

3. What style of instruction is Timothy to carefully avoid?

4. What is to be his focus instead?

5. What is it about Timothy that made him a kindred spirit to Paul?

# Lois and Eunice:
## *It Starts at Home*

WHEN WE BUY AN APPLE AT THE grocery store, we might say thank you to the cashier, but there were many hands working behind the scenes to provide the apple. A stock boy put the apples on the display. A trucker brought the apples from the warehouse. A picker put the apples into boxes. A farmer brought the crop to harvest. It may well be that a previous generation planted the trees. And of course, God supplied the sunshine and rain in the first place.

In like manner, when we are baptized into Christ, we might say thank you to the preacher who baptized us (if it was a preacher), but he was not the only one involved. The preacher was financially supported by others to be able to devote himself to teaching. The preacher learned the gospel from an older preacher, and he was encouraged by many other Christians to grow in his work. Perhaps he was influenced by others in the formative years of his life. And of course, God did the really heavy lifting of planning the gospel, providing the blood, broadcasting the message, and saving souls in the first place.

We have already studied what a diligent and effective preacher Timothy was. Paul says to Timothy,

> For I am mindful of the sincere faith within you, which first dwelt in your grandmother Lois and your mother Eunice, and I am sure that it is in you as well (2 Timothy 1:5).

Even in a united home, the efforts of Lois and Eunice would be remarkable. But Luke's comments in Acts 16:3 suggest that Timothy's father was not a believer, nor a big supporter of the faith. So, it's all the more special that Lois and Eunice saw to it that Timothy learned the stories of faith that helped Timothy develop a faith of his own. This speaks not to their ethnicity but their efforts. Faith is not passed down genetically, like wavy hair and blue eyes. It is passed down through influence. Lois and Eunice influenced Timothy. Paul said,

> You, however, continue in the things you have learned and become convinced of, knowing from whom you have learned them, and that from childhood you have known the sacred writings which are able to give you the wisdom that leads to salvation through faith which is in Christ Jesus. All Scripture is inspired by God and profitable for teaching, for reproof, for correction, for training in righteousness; so that the man of God may be adequate, equipped for every good work (2 Timothy 3:14–17).

The chain of Timothy's faith goes back generations. If no Lois, then no Eunice. If no Eunice, then no Timothy. Though salvation is of God (Psalm 3:8) from start to finish, each time Timothy taught a soul, Lois and Eunice could see the fruit of their influence. The world could use a lot more parents and grandparents like Lois and Eunice!

My wife and I are far from perfect parents. We're so far away from that ideal it makes us hang our heads. Still, we try our best to fulfill our God-given duty to "bring them up in the discipline and instruction of the Lord" (Ephesians 6:4) and we take that responsibility very seriously, knowing that we will stand in judgment of our efforts (Matthew 18:6; 1 Timothy 3:4–5). There are some dangerous things in life about which we offer zero leeway. We wouldn't watch from the kitchen window while our kids experiment with dynamite, saying, "Well, they have to learn for themselves." So it is with drugs, alcohol, the wrong crowd, and pornography. The spiritual damage done by these is huge and often irreparable. We set uncrossable negative boundaries in these areas.

But we also set some inflexible positive boundaries too; that is, not a list of things to avoid, but rather a list of formative experiences we want to make sure they *have*. For example, we absolutely require our kids to attend services, no exceptions for travel ball or birthday parties or the sniffles. This helps develop good habits and a sense of duty toward God, which will help them in those moments in adulthood when they will find themselves in a disappointing congregation or in difficult circumstances. We push our kids to attend gatherings of young Christians—things like our own local teen lunch studies and backyard sings, and things hosted elsewhere, like Florida College camps and teen challenge weekends. We organize our finances to prioritize these expenses. We cut back on eating in restaurants or the model of car we drive in order to have the money to pay for our kids to go to camp. We organize our schedules and adjust vacation dates to prioritize these events. We endure any inconvenience, driving long distances or missing sleep, to be sure our kids go. Here are five quick suggestions for being a modern Lois and Eunice:

**1. Exercise Authority**. It is the parents' job to exercise authority. Too many modern parents have wobbly spines. They want to be their kids' friends first, and parents second. Too often, when a kid shows the first signs of reluctance to go, they cave. Some of us have more courage to enforce a veggies-before-dessert rule than we do to enforce a church-gathering-before-movies rule! God has given parents the authority to say yes or no, and God demands they exercise it. If children don't learn the nature of inflexible authority from parents, they aren't likely to understand it in the workplace, or with regard to a Heavenly Father. Lay down reasonable rules; be unflinching and unapologetic in enforcing them. Don't worry about wanting children "to make up their own minds about God;" Satan will give them plenty of opportunities to rethink their faith as they grow older. Don't offer Satan equal time! Almost always, adult children will voice their appreciation for your forcing them to be faithful. They will, in turn, set many of the same rules for their own kids. That helps establish a heritage of faith lasting generations (Genesis 18:19). By the way, I figure that parents have until fifth grade to establish these habits. After that, it's too late to mold your children, and you'll have to reason with them as adults.

**2. Action Leads Them into a Better Way of Feeling.** I concede that watching *The Avengers* feels way more exciting than a campfire sing. Staying home to play video games spares a kid the awkwardness of interacting with new people face-to-face. So, expect your kids to be reluctant. Force your kids to go anyway. As with many things, they will learn to enjoy it after the experience of doing it. Soon, they will look forward to it!

**3. Teach Perspective Regarding the Wrong Crowd.** Teens *think* it's more fun to hang out with the wrong crowd (1 Corinthians 15:33). Only by being forced to hang out with Christians do they discover that young Christians are just as fun. Every person tends to emotionally invest in and develop close relationships with whomever they spend time with. See to it that a lot of that time is spent with young like-minded Christians.

**4. Relationships are Just as Important as Doctrine.** I realize that Bible teaching is essential for faith and strength. I realize that a Bible is more important than lunch and board games. But I have met *very* few people who fell away from the Lord because they heard a challenging sermon. I have known *very* many Christians who fell away because they didn't build close relationships with Christians.

**5. Do You Want Them to Marry a Christian, or Not?** Marrying a Christian is the second biggest decision one will ever make, and has more to do with whether or not one will go to heaven than anything else (I realize there are no guarantees, but the odds are higher). We don't arrange marriages in this day and age. So, parents must put children in situations where they can meet, grow to like, and fall in love with fellow Christians. That doesn't happen without intentional effort.

Lois and Eunice show how vital it is for families to pass down the faith. By the way, this is not the only place we recognize such a pattern. For example, Peter was a charismatic and influential member of the Apostles. He served as spokesman for the bunch at many points in Jesus' ministry. But sometimes we forget that it was his brother Andrew who brought him to see the Lord (John 1:35–42).

> Again the next day John was standing with two of his disciples, and he looked at Jesus as He walked, and said, "Behold, the Lamb of

God!" The two disciples heard him speak, and they followed Jesus. And Jesus turned and saw them following, and said to them, "What do you seek?" They said to Him, "Rabbi (which translated means Teacher), where are You staying?" He said to them, "Come, and you will see." So they came and saw where He was staying; and they stayed with Him that day, for it was about the tenth hour.

One of the two who heard John speak and followed Him, was Andrew, Simon Peter's brother. He found first his own brother Simon and said to him, "We have found the Messiah" (which translated means Christ). He brought him to Jesus. Jesus looked at him and said, "You are Simon the son of John; you shall be called Cephas" (which is translated Peter).

Andrew is not featured in the book of Acts like Peter. Andrew wrote no epistle that was preserved in the canon like Peter did. But Peter would never have done these things unless Andrew had been a faithful disciple of John the Baptist, had gone to spend time with Jesus, and then brought his brother Peter to come hear Jesus too.

Our congregations have a role to play. Paul says:

> The things which you have heard from me in the presence of many witnesses, entrust these to faithful men who will be able to teach others also (2 Timothy 2:2).

I started to preach because the congregation where I was baptized held open the sermon slots on the fifth Sundays for men of the congregation to preach. This was not to cover for the preacher's vacation time, but was intentionally set aside to develop the talents of the men of the congregation. I was prodded into putting my name down. I would not have done so otherwise. Thus, the gospel multiplies, as leaders and preachers identify others with the potential, and develop their skills and faith into the next generation of evangelists. Thanks be to Bible class teachers! And to congregations willing to endure beginner sermons!

# Questions for Thought

1. Whom does Paul recognize for molding Timothy's faith as a child?

2. If you are in Christ, who are some of the people who influenced you in that direction?

3. Does faith pass down from parent to child genetically?

4. What is one thing modern parents should do to help children develop a faith of their own?

5. One more thing?

# Silas:
## *Companion in a Dark Hour*

WHY DID JESUS SEND OUT both the twelve Apostles (Mark 6:7) and the seventy disciples (Luke 10:1) in pairs?

Perhaps, like swimming buddies at summer camp, it was to help with practical matters like injuries or illness on the road. Perhaps it was to guard against false accusations (2 Corinthians 13:1; Matthew 18:15–16). Perhaps it was so that money matters could be kept above board, "for we have regard for what is honorable, not only in the sight of the Lord, but also in the sight of men" (2 Corinthians 8:18–22).

Perhaps it was because Jesus knew, with the pressures and stresses of the work, with the persecutions His disciples would face, there would be times they needed to draw strength from one another, to keep one another in the faith.

In Acts 15, we first meet a man named Silas. He was one of the "leading men among the brethren" chosen by the apostles to go to Antioch with Paul and Barnabas in order to share the apostles' letter about Jews and Gentiles in the kingdom (Acts 15:22). While in Antioch, "Judas and Silas, being prophets themselves, encouraged and strengthened the brethren with a lengthy message" (Acts 15:32), and remained in Antioch for some time.

In Acts 15:40, Paul parted ways with Barnabas and John Mark. Paul chose Silas to come with him on his second missionary journey. Silas must have been a big part of Paul's efforts. He helped Paul reason in the synagogue in Thessalonica (Acts 17:4) and eventually fled with him by night to Berea (Acts 17:10). Soon Paul had to flee Berea too, but Silas remained there with Timothy to strengthen new churches (Acts 17:14). They finally reported back to Paul toward the end of the second journey (Acts 17:15; 18:5). Later, Paul mentions Silas' good work at Corinth (2 Corinthians 1:19). Silas is a cosigner of both Thessalonian letters (assuming, as most commentators do, that Silvanus is the Latinized form of Silas). Some suggest Silas was well-educated, since he is also mentioned as a helper and amanuensis to Peter (1 Peter 5:12).

But the most famous scene involving Silas happens in Philippi, after Paul had cast an evil spirit of divination out of a slave girl.

> But when her masters saw that their hope of profit was gone, they seized Paul and Silas and dragged them into the marketplace before the authorities, and when they had brought them to the chief magistrates, they said, "These men are throwing our city into confusion, being Jews, and are proclaiming customs which it is not lawful for us to accept or to observe, being Romans."
> The crowd rose up together against them, and the chief magistrates tore their robes off them and proceeded to order them to be beaten with rods. When they had struck them with many blows, they threw them into prison, commanding the jailer to guard them securely; and he, having received such a command, threw them into the inner prison and fastened their feet in the stocks.
> But about midnight, Paul and Silas were praying and singing hymns of praise to God, and the prisoners were listening to them; and suddenly there came a great earthquake, so that the foundations of the prison house were shaken; and immediately all the doors were opened and everyone's chains were unfastened (Acts 16:19–26).

I must imagine this was one of the most difficult moments of Paul's ministry. He had only just begun to answer the Macedonian call, God's own instructions to be there. He had only proclaimed Christ in Philippi only a matter of days (16:18). Still, he presented the gospel as the necessary alternative to the idols of the Greco-Roman Pantheon, and he was bold and successful enough to throw the city into confusion. Then, he rescued a slave-girl of an unclean spirit, which was clearly profitable for her owners, but horrible for her. In an instant, he found himself seized by a lawless mob, beaten with rods, and chained in the darkest, dankest part of the local Roman jail. Was God still blessing him, or not?

It sure feels better to have a companion in suffering. Paul's part in this ordeal must have been made more bearable by the presence of Silas. When Paul's ankles hurt, Silas could commiserate and cheer him up. When Paul experienced worry or doubt, Silas could remind him of their role. Together, they could brighten their situation by thinking of stories from the Old Testament prophets who endured, and by singing songs of God's greatness and faithfulness. I have no reason to think that Paul couldn't have survived this ordeal without Silas, but I'm also confident that Silas' presence was a huge source of encouragement.

It reminds me of this important passage:

> Two are better than one, because they have a good return for their labor. For if either of them falls, the one will lift up his companion. But woe to the one who falls when there is not another to lift him up. Furthermore, if two lie down together they keep warm, but how can one be warm alone? And if one can overpower him who is alone, two can resist him. A cord of three strands is not quickly torn apart (Ecclesiastes 4:9–12).

Brotherhood is such a God-given blessing, illustrated here in four ways: Brothers "have a good return for their labor." They contribute toward a common goal. They share insight, experience, and encouragement. Many hands make light work.

Brothers "lift up" a fallen companion. "A friend loves at all times, and a brother is born for adversity" (Proverbs 17:17). We conduct spiritual rescue missions. "If a man is caught in any trespass, you who are spiritual, restore such a one in a spirit of gentleness" (Galatians 6:1).

> My brethren, if any among you strays from the truth and one turns him back, let him know that he who turns a sinner from the error of

his way will save his soul from death and will cover a multitude of sins (James 5:19–20).

Brothers stay close and "keep warm." The church is a group in which each member can find strength and comfort when bad news comes, when sickness invades, when persecution draws near. Brothers are "made complete in the same mind and in the same judgment" (1 Corinthians 1:10).

And brothers share in the common defense. Peter reminds us that our "adversary, the Devil, prowls around like a roaring lion, seeking someone to devour" (1 Peter 5:8). In the wild, lions observe the flock from the high grass at the edge of the prairie, looking for weak or distracted stragglers who have wandered away from the group. They prefer isolated targets. Not even the king of the jungle will attack a tough knot of determined beasts, horns facing outward and ready to defend each other. When brothers stand together, Satan thinks twice. Perhaps this is why Paul writes to the same Christians where his ordeal occurred, hoping to hear that they were "standing firm in one spirit, with one mind striving together for the faith of the gospel, in no way alarmed by your opponents" (Philippians 1:27–28). Like a braided rope, all the fibers must be bound in unity.

Together, they endured. What a wonderful outcome their faith and joy provided to the lost of Philippi.

When the jailer awoke and saw the prison doors opened, he drew his sword and was about to kill himself, supposing that the prisoners had escaped. But Paul cried out with a loud voice, saying, "Do not harm yourself, for we are all here!"

And he called for lights and rushed in, and trembling with fear he fell down before Paul and Silas, and after he brought them out, he said, "Sirs, what must I do to be saved?"

They said, "Believe in the Lord Jesus, and you will be saved, you and your household." And they spoke the word of the Lord to him together with all who were in his house.

And he took them that very hour of the night and washed their wounds, and immediately he was baptized, he and all his household. And he brought them into his house and set food before them, and rejoiced greatly having believed in God with his whole household (Acts 16:27–34).

This night in prison was undoubtedly a long and difficult one for Paul, which God made more bearable with the presence of his fellow prisoner Silas. As a result of Paul and Silas' cheerfulness in pain, joy in suffering, and worship in darkness, the Roman jailer's heart was softened. Because Paul and Silas didn't flee when they had a chance, the Roman jailer's life was spared. Before the night was out, the Lord visited Philippi, and the Roman jailer and his household were brought out of their own darkness into the marvelous light!

## Questions for Thought

1.  What are some reasons disciples should still evangelize in pairs?

2.  What kind of person was Silas before he joined Paul on the second missionary journey?

3.  In what ways did Silas help the gospel work?

4.  How did Silas prove to be especially valuable to Paul in Philippi?

5.  What are some of the blessings of brotherhood mentioned in Ecclesiastes 4:9–12? How have you seen these things in your own life?

# Phoebe:
## *Servant of the Church*

PAUL WROTE ROMANS FROM CORINTH. At the close of the letter, as is customary, Paul acknowledged several people in Rome by name, and sent greetings from people on his end. But first Paul mentioned Phoebe. He does more than just send greetings:

> I commend to you our sister Phoebe, who is a servant of the church which is at Cenchrea; that you receive her in the Lord in a manner worthy of the saints, and that you help her in whatever matter she may have need of you; for she herself has also been a helper of many, and of myself as well (Romans 16:1–2).

Cenchrea was a tiny shoreside village just a stone's throw down the hill from Corinth. No doubt, Paul would have known the brethren in Cenchrea just as well as the brethren in Corinth.

Ralph Earle's *Word Meanings in the New Testament* suggests the word "commend to" is a technical term used in a letter of introduction. In this case, Paul vouches for Phoebe's character as a faithful Christian, a true "sister" in the family of God.

Maybe Phoebe was simply moving from Cenchrea to Rome, and Paul wanted her to be welcomed into a new congregation. But because Phoebe tops the lengthy list of people in Romans 16, and because he asks for their assistance "in whatever matter she may have need of you," it seems that she is on an errand from Paul. Many commentators believe Paul sent the Roman letter from Corinth to Rome in her hands. Perhaps Paul entrusted her to gather information about the situation in Rome (where Paul had not yet visited, Romans 1:10–15) and how his letter was received, and to return to Paul with a report; much as Chloe's people had sent a report to Paul about the situation in Corinth (1 Corinthians 1:11).

Does it surprise you to think that Paul would entrust an important job, whatever its actual nature, to a sister in the faith? It should not! Anyone who has read the New Testament understands that women are fellow heirs of the grace of life (1 Peter 3:7), that in Christ there is no distinction between male and female (Galatians 3:28). True, there are some limitations, and sisters in Christ must cultivate submissive hearts in light of 1 Timothy 2:11–15 and 1 Corinthians 14:34–35, as well as Ephesians 5:22–33, until the resurrection erases the temporary condition of gender (Matthew 22:30).

The Bible frequently mentions the contributions of women to the church. In his letters, Paul greets Mary "who has worked hard for you" (Romans 16:6), Tryphaena and Tryphosa who are "workers in the Lord," (Romans 16:12), and Euodia and Syntyche who "shared my struggle in the cause of the gospel" (Philippians 4:2–3). Clearly, women are not second-class citizens in the kingdom of God. Paul also praised the teaching that women do (2 Timothy 1:5; Titus 2:3–4). There are situations where it is inappropriate for a woman to teach (1 Timothy 2:11–12) and she will have to be careful not to exceed the position that God has granted her. The great commission is addressed to women, too. An established Christian woman has a host of skills and knowledge to pass along to young Christian women and those newly converted. She becomes the mother and sister to the new saint (Mark 10:28–31), who is often disentangling from worldly influences.

She can even evangelize. She is in the best position of all to preach the gospel to an unbelieving husband (1 Peter 3:1–2), and to both offer strength and voice concern to the struggling husband. Women in the New Testament directly supported the ministry of Christ (Luke 8:1–3). Women also hosted churches in their homes and provided a base of operations for Paul and his fellow workers, as did Lydia in Acts 16:15. They invited others to come and hear Jesus, as did the woman at the well (John 4:28–42).

It may very well be that women are braver than men when it comes to faith. E.S. Barrett points out, "Woman: last at the cross, first at the tomb." They were probably converted in greater numbers in all periods of history. In any case, they are equally valued by God (Galatians 3:28), and can look forward to an equal reward. Women were not exempt from torture in those days of persecution. The Roman official Pliny refers to two female Christians he had brutally tortured in order to extract information about local congregations.

Modern feminism is a repudiation of family, God, and biology, but Jesus' attitude toward women is elevating, respectful, and loving. Modern feminism's worst enemy is the family, and best friend is an intrusive government. But, Jesus counted women among his disciples "with Him" (Luke 8:1–3). Jesus appeared first to Mary Magdalene, and sent her, as some have said, *apostolorum apostola,* that is, "apostle to the apostles." Paul's first convert in Europe was found at a riverside gathering of women praying (Acts 16:14–15). Paul commended Priscilla, who helped her husband Aquila teach Apollos (Acts 18:26).

It's an interesting question whether Phoebe held the official title of "deaconess," as a few translations suggest. The word *diakonos* can mean deacon as an office (Philippians 1:1) requiring qualifications, or simply "servant" (Matthew 23:11; Romans 15:8). Most people are probably comfortable imagining her as a servant in the same sense that any Christian is a servant. At the same time, it's possible that the qualifications in 1 Timothy 3:11, "Women must likewise be dignified, not malicious gossips, but temperate, faithful in all things," may to refer to women who serve the church in an official capacity. Serving is not the same as leading, and thus viewing it that way causes no contradiction with passages like 1 Timothy 2:11. Now, traditionally, 1 Timothy 3:11 has been applied to wives of elders, but consider the following points:

- If Paul is referring to wives of any group, the rules of grammar suggest it would be wives of deacons, not wives of elders, since deacons are the subject of the proximate verses before and after verse 11. And why would there be qualifications for deacons' wives but not elders' wives?
- The word *gunaikas* means either "woman" or "wife," depending on the context.

- The word "their" is nowhere in the verse, and seems a stretch to supply it without a good reason.
- The Greek word that begins the sentence, *hosautos*, "likewise," signifies "a new class analogous to the preceding order" (Guthrie 97). First Paul gives qualifications for elders (1–7), then "likewise" qualifications for deacons (8), then "likewise" these women (11). This suggests verse 11 provides qualifications for new group analogous to the rest of those in the list—elders, deacons, then women who serve.

Whether or not a congregation wants to give these women who serve a title, we already ask women to serve in important roles as children's class teachers, planners of funeral food, and secretaries. Perhaps it would be wise to appoint women for those jobs who indeed are dignified, temperate, faithful in all things, and not malicious gossips.

I like how Ferrell Jenkins sums this up, in his book on *The Church* (p. 39):

> Many see a problem in saying that Phoebe was a deaconess. This, they think, would contradict 1 Timothy 2:11–15…. If we think of Phoebe and the women of 1 Timothy 3:11 as servants in the general sense, then no problem exists. Many women have served the church in this way.

Let's move on. In whatever capacity Phoebe served the Lord and served the church, her efforts made her "a helper of many." The Greek word *prostatis* appears only here in the New Testament. In Greek documents, it means "patron, succorer, protector" (Earle, *Word Meanings in the New Testament*, 213). Perhaps Phoebe was a woman of means, and may have helped Paul financially, as the women of Luke 8:1–3. Perhaps she acted like the Barnabas of Cenchrea, or surrounding congregations, like the good woman of Proverbs 31:20. Perhaps she performed acts of kindness for her brethren, like Tabitha in Acts 9:36–41. Perhaps she comforted those in distress (1 Timothy 5:10). I'd like to think she did a little of everything!

Finally, Phoebe was among the "saints." All Christians are supposed to be saints, for "saint" simply describes one who is holy unto the Lord. Phoebe's behavior was righteous and clean. Her name in Greek means "pure, radiant." In fact, in the Roman world this was the name given to a goddess of the moon, which shines with a silvery, brilliant light. Phoebe certainly was a light to the world! She could be recognized by all as a true Christian.

## Questions for Thought

1. What are some theories for why Paul commended Phoebe to the Roman saints, that they receive her in a worthy manner and help her?

2. What are some theories for how Phoebe was a helper of Paul and many others?

3. What is the range of meanings to understand Phoebe as a "servant"?

4. Are women hard workers in the church, with many responsibilities?

5. What is your own understanding of the group whose qualifications are given in 1 Timothy 3:11?

# Philemon and Onesimus:
## *Made Useful in Christ*

THE STORY OF ONESIMUS AND PHILEMON is much more dramatic than it first seems.

Paul addresses this very short letter

> …to Philemon our beloved brother and fellow worker, and to Apphia our sister, and to Archippus our fellow soldier, and to the church in your house (Philemon 1–2).

Many believe these three were part of the same family. Comparing these names to those in the Colossian letter, it seems clear that Philemon and his family lived in Colossae. Perhaps the church meeting in Philemon's home was the Colossian church, or perhaps a nearby church. Paul probably sent these two letters at the same time, in the hands of Tychicus and Onesimus (Colossians 4:7–9).

Paul speaks of how much "joy and comfort" he received from Philemon. In fact, it's one of my favorite meditations anywhere, when Paul says, "the hearts of the saints have been refreshed through you, brother" (7). May we all strive to refresh our brethren by our words and our deeds! Clearly, Paul felt like Philemon was a guy he could depend on, who was a blessing to brethren near and far.

Paul quickly turns to the matter of Onesimus, which takes up the bulk of the letter. It soon becomes clear that Onesimus was a slave (16). It also becomes clear, reading between the lines, that Onesimus at some point in the past had run away from his master, who was none other than Philemon. And it becomes clear, though this may shock you a bit, that Paul was sending Onesimus back to his owner!

Sometimes, people get upset to discover that slavery is not flatly condemned in the New Testament. I would argue that the word of Jesus paved the way for the eventual abolition of slavery and the founding of nations in which all are treated as social equals in God's sight. The gospel was not primarily designed to bring about political revolution or economic justice, but rather eternal salvation despite one's earthly circumstances. Thus, God's message to slaves was to be godly slaves (Ephesians 6:5–9; Colossians 3:22–25; 1 Timothy 6:1–8; 1 Peter 2:13–24). God's message to slave owners was to be kind, and to recognize them as people with a Master in heaven (Ephesians 6:9, Colossians 4:1).

It may mitigate the disappointment to learn that slavery in first-century Rome was different than our recent American experience. Some historians estimate that about 30% of the inhabitants of the Roman Empire were of the slave class. Slaves came from conquered peoples, or from the ranks of the poor, who sometimes indentured themselves voluntarily for financial reasons. Slaves could be better fed and more stable than free landowners. See for example *Civilization of the Ancient Mediterranean,* Vol. 1, p. 584, and *Cambridge Ancient History,* Vol. 10, p. 756, and 80. While most slaves performed manual labor, some also were highly educated to do secretarial work and accounting, play music, teach children, and serve as doctors. I'm not by any means suggesting it was a desirable life—a slave was the property of the master, and Romans could be very harsh to their slaves. In fact, Paul urges Christians to become free if possible, and never to indenture themselves, for it would make it more difficult to serve God (1 Corinthians 7:21–24). The attitude of racial inferiority, upon which our American experience of slavery was often rationalized, is condemned in Scripture (Mark 16:15-16; Acts 10:34; 2 Corinthians 5:16; Colossians 3:11; Revelation 5:9). Still, the kingdom of God is about changing people's hearts one at a time, rather than overthrowing societies. Christ's message to Roman slaves was to not worry about changing things they could not change, but to glorify God through their service, and to submit to the laws of the land.

Thus, in his historical context, Onesimus had defrauded his master by running away. And so, though it may run counter to our sense of justice, Paul sent Onesimus back to Philemon.

But Paul sent him back with a plea.

> I appeal to you for my child Onesimus, whom I have begotten in my imprisonment, who formerly was useless to you, but now is useful both to you and to me. I have sent him back to you in person, that is, sending my very heart, whom I wished to keep with me, so that on your behalf he might minister to me in my imprisonment for the gospel; but without your consent I did not want to do anything, so that your goodness would not be, in effect, by compulsion but of your own free will. For perhaps he was for this reason separated from you for a while, that you would have him back forever, no longer a slave, but more than a slave, a beloved brother, especially to me, but how much more to you, both in the flesh and in the Lord (Philemon 10–16).

It seems that Onesimus ran away from Philemon, bumped into Paul, learned the gospel, and became a Christian. Paul suggests that there many have been more going on than mere chance.

Paul is careful to say "perhaps," the language of providence. God created the world, and God sustains the world, but not every occurrence should be chalked up to the direct action of God. He is able to change things as big as the movement of planets (Joshua 10:13) and as small as the path of a sparrow (Matthew 10:29) or the meal of a worm (Jonah 4:7), but the world largely operates on rules of physics, chemistry, and biology that God established. Sometimes God enters the world miraculously, in obvious "signs and wonders," designed to incontrovertibly draw man's attention to His word (Hebrews 2:3–4). He fulfills prophecy (John 19:11), and He changes lives (Galatians 1:15).

But not every red light or green light, not every flight delay, not every doctor visit, is a direct act of God. Some are just coincidences (Ecclesiastes 9:11). We go astray when we try to assign meaning to everything. Have you heard the one about the man who was on a diet? He prayed that God would help him pass by the donut shop, but that if the parking spot directly in front of the entrance was open, he would interpret it as a sign from God for him to pull in and grab a donut. He only circled the block twenty times before the spot was open! How silly, but how many times have we credited God with "opening a door" to allow us to buy a car that proved too expensive, or "directing our footsteps" to an activity that proved unhealthy?

In fact, we must be very careful, because some coincidences could be from Satan. Someone very close to me was on vacation a thousand miles from home. Suddenly, he bumped into an old high school flame. He rationalized that God Himself must have brought them together—how else to explain the odds of such a meeting! He divorced his wife of thirty years to be with the old flame. I guarantee, it was not a sign from God. It may have been Satan, or it may have been a bizarre coincidence, but it was not God. No vision, feeling, or odd circumstance trumps the revealed word of God (Deuteronomy 13:1–5; Colossians 2:18; Galatians 1:6–9).

So, Paul says that "perhaps" Onesimus ran into Paul because God was bending his path to encounter the gospel, so that he would have the opportunity to be saved. God can even use a sinful action, like a theft of property, while not causing the sinful action, to bring about a good result. Like Mordecai said of Esther, "Who knows whether you have not attained royalty for such a time as this?" (Esther 4:14).

If so, this is a wonderful way that God providentially provided. Our congregation supports preachers in Nicaragua. Not long ago I was reading a letter from an American preacher trying to get the funds to go and help. Two weeks before the trip, he was still $1,800 short of his funding. He sent out requests and prayed, deciding if God wanted him to go, he'd get the funding; if not, he'd cancel. The very next day (meaning that the requests were still at the post office) a check arrived for exactly $1,800 and none of the requests were ever answered. A miracle? No. A coincidence? Possibly, but I doubt it. I couldn't prove it with the scientific method, but it seems to me it was God answering prayer through providence. Let's get in the habit of thanking God when things work out for a godly result.

Paul hoped that Philemon would receive Onesimus in forgiveness and kindness, thinking of his departure as a providential way for him to obey the gospel. In fact, Paul even offered to repay damages caused by Onesimus (18). This new relationship meant that everything changes. Now, Onesimus was a saint. Now he was a beloved brother. Now he was useful not just in the flesh as a slave, but in the Lord as a member of the body of Christ. In fact, Paul purposefully played on the meaning of Onesimus' name. In Greek it means "useful." One might expect it to be a very common name for a household slave. Paul suggested that as a non-Christian slave, Onesimus wasn't nearly as "useful" to Philemon as he would be now, coming back to Philemon as a Christian, who could build him up in the Lord. In Christ, he could truly live up to his name.

If Philemon had the ability, and the duty, to forgive Philemon for running away and defrauding him, then surely we Christians can forgive one another for the slights we inflict upon one another today.

Paul makes another request of Philemon, that he would allow Onesimus to return to Paul to minister to him in his imprisonment. Paul didn't presume to do this without Philemon's permission. But if Philemon followed through, this would be a way that Philemon himself could have fellowship with Paul's gospel work.

Let us see the true value of those in our circles of acquaintances. I've always thought it was a shame that Onesimus had to flee Philemon and bump into Paul to learn the gospel. Maybe I'm being too harsh on Philemon; maybe Philemon *did* teach Onesimus about Jesus, and Onesimus sought out Paul on purpose, who provided the extra nudge he needed to obey the gospel. Who knows! In any case, don't shield your mechanic, your doctor, your teacher from the gospel, because you don't want to "ruin" your friendly relationship. If you have employees, it's counterproductive to coerce them into faith, but always think of them as prospects for the gospel. How much more wonderful it could be to have Christian employees!

# Questions for Thought

1. What wonderful action did Paul thank Philemon for?

2. What was Onesimus to Philemon before the circumstances described in the letter? What was he after?

3. Why did Paul send Onesimus back to Philemon?

4. What does Paul ask Philemon to do?

5. In what ways are brethren "useful" to one another?

# Archippus:
## *Fulfilling His Ministry*

WHEN PAUL ADDRESSES THE BRIEF LETTER to Philemon, he greets other people, too:

> …to Philemon our beloved brother and fellow worker, and to Apphia our sister, and to Archippus our fellow soldier, and to the church in your house (Philemon 1–2).

Some believe that Apphia is Philemon's wife, and Archippus his son or brother. They lived in Colossae. It seems likely that the church in Philemon's house was, in fact, the Colossian congregation, or at least one of them. A comparison of the proper names in the letters to Philemon and Colossae suggests Paul wrote and sent both letters at the same time. In the letter to the Colossians, Paul says:

> Say to Archippus: "Take heed to the ministry which you have received in the Lord, that you may fulfill it" (Colossians 4:17).

Note that Paul had *addressed* Archippus by name in the other letter. He could have said what he wanted to say to Archippus there while he had his attention. Presumably, Paul wanted this statement to be read not just by Archippus and his family, but read and even echoed by the whole Colossian church!

Paul mentions three things in this short sentence: what Archippus had, who gave it to him, and what to do with it.

First, Archippus had a ministry. Christians should stop being afraid of the word "ministry." It simply means "work of service." In some contexts it means the work of a deacon or the work of an apostle (Acts 1:17; 2 Corinthians 5:18), even the work of an angel (Hebrews 1:14). In some contexts it refers to the preaching of the gospel (Acts 20:24; 2 Corinthians 6:3). But it just as well refers to serving food (Luke 10:40; Acts 6:1) and gathering financial support for the suffering (2 Corinthians 9:1; Romans 15:31). Many times, like here in Colossians 4:17, the exact nature of the ministry is not fleshed out. "There are a variety of ministries, but the same Lord" (1 Corinthians 12:5). "The household of Stephanas … have devoted themselves for ministry to the saints" (1 Corinthians 16:15). "I know your deeds, and your love and faith and service and perseverance" (Revelation 2:19).

In short, a ministry is a broad term referring to work done to serve other people. Archippus had a ministry. He knew what it was. His ministry could have been serving as an evangelist, preaching the gospel and strengthening the brethren in Colossae while Epaphras was away. His ministry could have been preaching at one of the neighboring towns, such as Laodicea. His ministry could have been simply feeding the widows of the Colossian church, or organizing the children's Bible classes. Any of these, or all of these and more.

The word "minister" is a title most of us would rather pay someone else to wear. But "minister" simply means "one who serves." Thus, every Christian is by definition a minister. Every Christian has a duty to serve in some area.

> And He gave some as apostles, and some as prophets, and some as evangelists, and some as pastors and teachers, for the equipping of the saints for the work of service, to the building up of the body of Christ; until we all attain to the unity of the faith, and of the knowledge of the Son of God, to a mature man, to the measure of the stature which belongs to the fullness of Christ (Ephesians 4:11–13).

Jesus Himself provided the teaching ministries to equip the body of Christ for further works of ministry. When every saint performs some "work of service" as a minister, the body of Christ grows strong and healthy. In fact, it is vital for every Christian to find a ministry. Churches often discover that there are many ministries that need to happen that cannot happen unless God provides a minister, someone with the talent and willingness to serve.

An internet ministry cannot happen without a person who learns how to build and maintain a webpage. A widow-care ministry cannot happen without a person to organize and assign the work, and ministers to cook and clean. A quality Bible class ministry cannot happen without a person to recruit and train teachers, assign curriculum, and check on classes.

Second, Jesus is the one who gave Archippus his ministry; it was "received in the Lord." Every minister must realize that his ministry is entrusted to him by Jesus Christ, and it is to Jesus Christ that he must be faithful. It's not a job, it's not a hobby, it's a ministry, to bring others closer to maturity in Christ.

A deacon might ask you to teach the three-year-old Bible class, but Jesus gives you the talents to perform that ministry, and the responsibility to carry out that ministry. An elder might ask you to lead songs, but Jesus gives you the talents to perform that ministry, and the responsibility to carry out that ministry. You yourself might set your mind to preach, but Jesus gives you the talents to perform that ministry, and the responsibility to carry out that ministry.

Remembering that we work for the Lord really helps ride out the bumps and lulls and discouragement that inevitably threaten all ministries. Christians who are trying to serve from time to time get jaded and upset. Why keep working when people complain, when people forget to say thank you, when people drag their feet? Ministers keep working because ministers report to Jesus, not to the members of the church. Ultimately, ministers do not take on their projects because they so enjoy what they are doing (though hopefully they do) or because they receive such praise (though hopefully they do). They keep at it because they strive to be faithful to Jesus. They conceive of their ministry as a job given to them by Jesus Himself.

Perhaps the individuals who need to take this to heart the most are full-time preachers. The way most modern congregations function on a day-to-day basis makes it quite easy for a preacher to keep the members satisfied. He can throw together an outline or two on Saturday night, he can deliver them with charisma on Sunday morning, and cash his support check and claim the rest of the week as his own free time. In fact, he may even receive praise for "standing for the truth." Sadly, this is one major reason why many congregations are in decline—the preacher hasn't focused on his God-given ministry in a long time. The preacher may have hoodwinked the largely-uninvolved members of the congregation, but he will still have to give an account of Himself to God. If he considers God to be his boss, he wouldn't dare turn in such shoddy work. As Paul said to Timothy:

> But you, be sober in all things, endure hardship, do the work of an evangelist, fulfill your ministry (2 Timothy 4:5).

Third, Paul publicly encourages Archippus to "take heed" to his ministry, that he may "fulfill it." Paul uses the same word of his own ministry in Colossians 1:25. Archippus should be diligent in his ministry, not to mark time, but to accomplish the end goal of glorifying Jesus.

Whatever ministry Jesus gives us, let us perform it to our maximum effort. Don't worry about fulfilling someone else's ministry. Don't worry so much about riches and the cares of life that you forget about your ministry. Fulfill your ministry.

Parents, take heed to your ministry. God has given you the job of feeding, training, correcting, and loving your children. They won't be under your wing long. Fulfill your ministry.

Bible class teachers, take heed to your ministry. God has given you the job of passing along the lessons of the Scriptures to the most impressionable minds. God has given you the talent to love them and communicate with them. Come prepared to every class. Be there early to greet them with a smile. Go above and beyond with visual aids and illustrations. Fulfill your ministry.

Deacons, take heed to your ministry. God has appointed you to serve the brethren in various mundane but important ways. Those who serve well obtain standing and confidence (1 Timothy 3:13). If the building is your area, see to it that the building is clean and in good repair. Failing to supervise the lawn service or the locksmith isn't just annoying, it's forgetting that Jesus gave you a ministry, and it results in visitors drawing negative conclusions by seeing things in a state of disrepair. If the teens are your area, don't let faithless and thankless parents discourage you, but see their growing faith as your God-given opportunity, and help these families grow as a result of your ministry. If the worship duty list is your area, have it done happily, in an organized fashion, well in advance, and don't become disgruntled when a number of men prove hesitant to sign up or negligent in showing up. Fulfill your ministry.

Elders, take heed to your ministry. Leadership is perhaps the biggest need in the church today. Have monthly meetings to discuss the work of the church, pray for each member by name, track down the missing sheep, find ways to reach the community with the gospel. Fulfill your ministry.

Each and every member, take heed to your ministry. If it's providing food, do so with joy. If it's writing cards, do so with regularity. Whatever it is, fulfill your ministry. And if you aren't currently devoting yourself to a ministry, it's past time to find one.

# Questions for Thought

1. Why might Paul have presented his exhortation to Archippus in the broader Colossian letter, rather than the more intimate letter to Philemon?

2. Why are some reluctant to speak of "ministry"? Are you a minister?

3. Who gave Archippus his ministry?

4. What did Paul want Archippus to do with his ministry?

5. What is your ministry, and how can you fulfill it this week?

# Phygelus and Hermogenes, Demas, John Mark: *Those Who Quit*

IN THIS SERIES, WE HAVE so far looked only at positive examples. There are negative lessons to be learned from a few names, too.

Toward the end of his life, Paul was in a Roman prison, awaiting trial on a capital offense. It seems that this time, Paul expected a guilty verdict and execution. Paul bravely faced his fate, determined to complete his task of proclaiming the death burial and resurrection of Jesus.

At such a stressful time, it would be mighty helpful to be surrounded by throngs of supporters. Or at least a handful. Paul had no such blessings. He testified sadly,

> You are aware of the fact that all who are in Asia turned away from me, among whom are Phygelus and Hermogenes.
>
> At my first defense no one supported me, but all deserted me; may it not be counted against them. But the Lord stood with me and strengthened me, so that through me the proclamation might be fully accomplished, and that all the Gentiles might hear; and I was rescued out of the lion's mouth (2 Timothy 1:15; 4:16–17).

What a heartbreaking situation, to stand friendless and alone before the Roman magistrates, having to be brave and outspoken while bottling up the sadness of being abandoned. Thankfully, Paul knew that while people often prove to be less than dependable, Christ never abandons his children!

Let me say this very strongly: human beings are imperfect. The church is designed to be a nurturing, loving, supportive, wholesome, smiling family.

Most of the time, it is. But even the best Christians will disappoint you sooner or later.

It is essential that every Christian, but especially those who serve as elders, teachers, and preachers, prepare themselves for disappointment. A fellow elder will be accused of infidelity. A majority of a congregation will not respond well to a needful message, and will harshly criticize or even call for a change in the preacher. A dear Christian friend you thought the world of will suffer an emotional loss and fall away.

This passage may sound strong, but it's applicable:

> Thus says the Lord,
> "Cursed is the man who trusts in mankind
> And makes flesh his strength,
> And whose heart turns away from the Lord.
> For he will be like a bush in the desert
> And will not see when prosperity comes,
> But will live in stony wastes in the wilderness,
> A land of salt without inhabitant.
> Blessed is the man who trusts in the Lord
> And whose trust is the Lord.
> For he will be like a tree planted by the water,
> That extends its roots by a stream
> And will not fear when the heat comes;
> But its leaves will be green,
> And it will not be anxious in a year of drought
> Nor cease to yield fruit" (Jeremiah 17:5–8).

Your faith and service must never be based on the faith and service of others. You cannot control what other people do, but you can control your reaction to what other people do. Never falter! Never change your moral foundation because someone else changes his or her moral foundation.

So much depends on it! What if Paul stormed out of the Corinthian church, never to return, because he faced examples of immorality? What if Paul cancelled the second missionary journey because he couldn't agree with Barnabas? What if Paul allowed himself a little sin in his life because he saw Peter and even Barnabas (not even Barnabas a perfect Son of Encouragement!) allow a little hypocrisy in their lives (Galatians 2:11–14)? What if Paul threw in the towel and went into retirement because he faced dangers from false brethren (2 Corinthians 11:26)? Just think of all the good that would have been lost!

Jesus is not a fickle friend. If a government thug blocked entry to the church house, we would give up our very lives to stay true to Jesus. Why then would we allow a struggling Christian's hypocrisy prevent us from worshiping God? Some of Satan's most successful attacks come from within the body, not without. Determine that everywhere you go you will be part of the solution, not part of the problem.

### Demas: He Loved This Present World
Another who disappointed Paul was Demas.

> Make every effort to come to me soon; for Demas, having loved this present world, has deserted me and gone to Thessalonica; Crescens has gone to Galatia, Titus to Dalmatia. Only Luke is with me (2 Timothy 4:9-11).

Once, years earlier, Demas had been listed among Paul's fellow workers (Colossians 4:14). But the kingdom of the Lord can be difficult and require sacrifices. For every Timothy and Titus who serve faithfully and endure to the end, there are others who have a change of heart. Perhaps Demas just wasn't prepared for the hectic schedule of travel Paul would demand, or the challenges of speaking out boldly. But then again, we have seen so many modern Christians who are not even willing to give up a few illicit pleasures for the privilege of knowing Christ, who are not even willing to wake up on Sunday morning for the joy of meeting Jesus!

Whether we are a one-talent or a five-talent person, whether we are called to serve in an easy place or a hard place, the root cause of giving up is always the same—we love the world more than we love Jesus. We desire the "passing pleasures of sin" over eternal glory. We fail to keep our eyes fixed on the prize of heaven. Beware:

> If anyone wishes to come after Me, he must deny himself, and take up his cross and follow me. For whoever wishes to save his life will lose it, but whoever loses his life for My sake and the gospel's sake will save it. For what does it profit a man to gain the whole world, and forfeit his soul? (Mark 8:34–37).

### John Mark: He Left, but He Came Back
Early on Paul's first missionary journey, when Paul and Barnabas had evangelized Cyprus, they sailed for Asia Minor. But as soon as they touched the mainland, "John left them and returned to Jerusalem" (Acts 13:13).

This Mark is an early disciple and close associate of Peter (1 Peter 5:13), in whose mother's home the disciples met for prayer (Acts 12:12). He had one successful trip with Paul and Barnabas (Acts 12:25). He is likely the author of the gospel of Mark, which many believe draws heavily from Peter's eyewitness testimony. I don't get the impression that John Mark totally left the faith, but he certainly left Paul and Barnabas in the lurch. Was the schedule of preaching too difficult? Was opposition from Elymas too frightening? Was he just homesick? In any case, Paul took it as evidence of unreliability, so that later, at the beginning of the second missionary journey,

> Barnabas wanted to take John, called Mark, along with them also. But Paul kept insisting they should not take him along who had deserted them in Pamphylia and had not gone with them to the work. And there occurred such a sharp disagreement that they separated from one another, and Barnabas took Mark with him and sailed away to Cyprus. But Paul chose Silas and left (Acts 15:37–40).

Thankfully we can end our look at those who left on a high note. For we see that John Mark grew in faith, and proved diligent in service with Barnabas on Cyprus. In fact, many years later, John Mark is associated with Paul's work. Paul says to Timothy, "Pick up Mark and bring him with you, for he is useful to me for service" (2 Timothy 4:11; *cf.* Philemon 24).

If Jesus experienced disappointment, so shall we. As His crucifixion drew near, Jesus said to His disciples, "You will all fall away because of Me this night, for it is written … 'The sheep of the flock shall be scattered' (Matthew 26:31). But Jesus also pointed out that they would be reunited in Galilee, and would go on to do greater works. In Christ, what's broken can be repaired, and one who leaves may return. If you feel your faith flagging, draw nearer to Christ, before it is too late!

# Questions for Thought

1. Why do human beings eventually let us down?

2. What was the root cause of Demas' abandoning Paul?

3. Have you ever experienced a time of flagging faith? How did it affect others who were depending on you?

4. Has a brother in Christ ever behaved in such a way that shook your faith? What did you do to remain faithful to Christ?

5. Who will never let us down?

# Hymenaeus and Alexander, Philetus, Ananias and Sapphira, Diotrephes: *Those Who Did Harm*

I HAVE A FRIEND WHO MANAGES PROPERTIES. Some tenants fail to pay the rent and are required to move. Some tenants fail to pay the rent, but before they move, kick holes in the walls and pour cement in the toilets.

In the previous chapter, we looked at examples of men who abandoned Paul and abandoned Jesus. There are others who broke things on the way out, whose negative influence threatened Jesus' disciples.

Paul told Timothy,

> [Keep] faith and a good conscience, which some have rejected and suffered shipwreck in regard to their faith. Among these are Hymenaeus and Alexander, whom I have handed over to Satan, so that they will be taught not to blaspheme (1 Timothy 1:19–20).

I feel confident in stating that Hymenaeus and Alexander had once been faithful servants (though it's impossible to know if it's the same Alexander in Acts 19:33). After all, you have to be aboard the boat to have a shipwreck. The false doctrine "Once Saved Always Saved" is still believed by many, despite the host of passages which discuss the possibility and reality of a Christian falling away (Galatians 5:1–4; 1 Corinthians 8:11; 9:24–25; 10:12; 2 Peter 2:1–2; 2:20–21; Revelation 22:19; Acts 8:13–24; James 5:19–20; Hebrews 6:4–6; 10:26–31; Luke 8:13; and especially Ezekiel 33:13–16).

Not satisfied to wreck their own ship, Hymenaeus and Alexander also threatened to draw others to the same dangerous shoals. Paul identifies their sin as blasphemy. In Greek, *blasphemia* means "to injure one's reputation or good name." Paul uses the Greek root *blasphemia* in Romans 3:8;

Colossians 3:8; and Titus 3:2 to refer to slandering people. Today, we might call this sort of thing "libel," issuing a statement about someone that is untrue and is designed to harm him, to defame his character.

When one blasphemes God, he speaks falsely and slanderously against God's character (Luke 22:65; Matthew 27:39; Acts 13:45; 26:11; Romans 2:24; James 2:6–7). Hymenaeus and Alexander didn't just slip up and use the name of God in a vulgar or flippant way in conversation (though, this too is a serious thing, Exodus 20:7; Leviticus 24:10–16). They probably taught that Jesus was less than who He claimed to be, the Christ the Son of God, and thus blasphemed and caused others to waver in their faith.

Years later, we get another mention of Alexander (assuming it's the same man):

> Alexander the coppersmith did me much harm; the Lord will repay him according to his deeds. Be on guard against him yourself, for he vigorously opposed our teaching (2 Timothy 4:14–15).

As well as another mention of Hymenaeus:

> Avoid worldly and empty chatter, for it will lead to further ungodliness, and their talk will spread like gangrene. Among them are Hymenaeus and Philetus, men who have gone astray from the truth saying that the resurrection has already taken place, and they upset the faith of some (2 Timothy 2:16–18).

It's a tricky situation, to be forced to deal with a church member who sins. We want to reach out in mercy and gently rebuke those who are honestly struggling (James 5:19–20; Jude 22–23; etc.). But sometimes more drastic measures must be taken against those actively harming the work of the church. Extreme cases can require withdrawing fellowship. Hymenaeus and Alexander were leading others astray, and so Paul "handed them over to Satan," which seems to mean put out of the church and back into the world.

There are four reasons found in the Bible for removing a brother from the body of Christ: gross and unrepentant sin (1 Corinthians 5:1–13), undisciplined living (2 Thessalonians 3:6–15), false teaching (2 John 9–11), and factious behavior (Titus 3:10; Romans 16:17).

There are two goals in removing a brother from the body of Christ: To obtain the salvation of the individual (1 Corinthians 5:5) and to maintain the purity of the church (1 Corinthians 5:6–8; Deuteronomy 13:5). A church must be strong in the face of such faithlessness, lest many souls be destroyed by it.

### Diotrephes

On the other hand, refusing fellowship can be used in such a way to make leaders of the church feel puffed up. The Apostle John testifies:

> I wrote something to the church; but Diotrephes, who loves to be first among them, does not accept what we say. For this reason, if I come, I will call attention to his deeds which he does, unjustly accusing us with wicked words; and not satisfied with this, he himself does not receive the brethren, either, and he forbids those who desire to do so and puts them out of the church (3 John 9–10).

This man Diotrephes rejected apostolic authority, and loved "to be first," that is, was full of pride and drunk on power. This is not the humble leadership of a true shepherd, and this is not caring for the souls of the wayward. This is feeling important by imposing declarations.

Some are more willing to ruin a church than to allow others to rule it. I've heard it said that some churches will never grow until there are a few funerals. That's sad for a lot of reasons; but something as important as evangelism shouldn't have to wait for a terminal illness. People mustn't bow to such bullying. Oppose such men openly for the good of the church. Be willing as a congregation to suffer the loss of his contribution—it's best for the long term health of the church, for it will never grow numerically or spiritually under his thumb. He must face a united front of church members who are willing to stand up to such a person, who insist on directing the church in the right way.

**Ananias and Sapphira**
Finally, the book of Acts records an example where God Himself provided the discipline.

Ananias and Sapphira had seen Barnabas get a lot of attention for selling land and contributing it to the Lord (Acts 4:36–37). They wanted the same attention.

> [He] kept back some of the price for himself, with his wife's full knowledge, and bringing a portion of it, he laid it at the apostles' feet. But Peter said, "Ananias, why has Satan filled your heart to lie to the Holy Spirit and to keep back some of the price of the land? While it remained unsold did it not remain your own? And after it was sold, was it not under your control? Why is it that you have conceived this deed in your heart? You have not lied to men but to God." As he heard these words, Ananias fell down and breathed his last; and great fear came over all who heard of it (Acts 5:2–5).

Just a few hours later, the same tragic confrontation happened with Sapphira.

Now, their sin is often mischaracterized as stinginess. But Peter emphasizes that they could have given as much as they wanted; the full price of the land, half the price of the land, or even none at all. Deception was their sin. They acted as if their contribution was the full price of the land, when they had in fact lied and pocketed a percentage of the proceeds. In fact, the word "kept back" is translated in Titus 2:10 as "pilfering."

An otherwise–wonderful deed can be spoiled by an underlying lack of integrity. Some years ago, I was told a story about a couple who went to a fast food restaurant and got chicken sandwiches to go. They paid the bill, accepted the bag from the clerk, and headed out the door. Walking over to a nearby park, they opened the bag and discovered a wad of money and receipts. They realized there had been some mistake, and promptly returned to the restaurant and called for the manager. The manager of course was shocked. He had been in the habit of putting the daily deposits in a fast food bag when taking them to the bank, to fool would-be thieves. Somehow the bags had been switched, and the couple got a bag full of cash. The manager's shock quickly turned to happy amazement. The manager said, "I'm going to call the newspaper. You guys should be recognized for being so honest. You are the most honest people I've ever met!" The couple refused. The manager assumed they were being humble and deflecting praise, and picked up the phone. Finally the man asked to speak to the manager in his office. There, he said, "Look, we don't want to be in the paper." The manager kept on, "But this is a great story. It will inspire everyone else!" Finally the man explained, "The woman I am with is not my wife, if you catch my drift. We can't be in the paper. Please drop this."

A great deed had been done, but it was spoiled by a lack of integrity. And sin among Christians can have serious consequences. "Your sin will find you out" (Numbers 32:23). "Those who continue in sin, rebuke in the presence of all, so that the rest also will be fearful of sinning" (1 Timothy 5:20).

Because God dealt with this openly, the rest of the church reverently feared God, and immediately after, "All the more believers in the Lord, multitudes of men and women, were constantly added to their number" (Acts 5:14).

# Questions for Thought

1. What is the meaning of blasphemy, and why is it so awful?

2. Who suffered as a result of Hymenaeus, Alexander, and Philetus?

3. What reasons might a church have to withdraw fellowship from a brother?

4. What caution does the example of Diotrephes provide?

5. Why did God make an example of Ananias and Sapphira?

# Miscellany

THERE ARE MANY MORE NAMES that I skipped over, because the text doesn't say quite enough about them for me to draw four-page lessons. But the Holy Spirit sees fit to include them, so they are all special in their own way. They were known by sight to the original audience, and they shall one day be known by sight to us.

Besides, "time will fail" if we attempt to explore every person whose name appears. Think of all the drama *not* recorded in Acts; the others known to Paul and his fellow workers, who helped him and spread the gospel in their own ways, who made their own gigantic sacrifices, whose names are not recorded in the Bible at all, "of whom the world is not worthy." Their names are, however, written in the book of life (Luke 10:20) and the fruit of their labors live on.

For this last chapter, I scanned Acts through Jude and jotted down all the other "minor" Christians not discussed previously, with a short meditation on each. [All bold emphasis in the quoted scriptures are mine, John Guzzetta]

> The first account I composed, **Theophilus**, about all that Jesus began to do and teach (Acts 1:1).

The roots of Theophilus mean "lover of God," which could be his real name, or just a figurative and hopeful way for Luke to address his whole audience.

> So they put forward two men, Joseph called **Barsabbas** (who was also called Justus) and Matthias. And they prayed and said, "You Lord, who know the hearts of men, show which one of these two You have chosen to occupy this ministry" (Acts 1:23–26).

When a modern congregation appoints elders, there isn't a limited number of available positions—every man who is qualified can and should serve. But there was only the twelfth spot open for a new Apostle, and thus it was necessary to draw lots.

Poor Barsabbas—the Apostle who almost was. I feel for him like I feel for the losing team in the Super Bowl—so close, and yet so far! While nothing more is said of Barsabbas (he is not the Justus of Acts 18:7 or Colossians 4:11), I like to think that Luke's silence indicates he didn't pitch a fit, but found other important ways to serve God in the kingdom. Let us not regret the opportunities we don't have, but take full advantage of the opportunities God provides.

> …they chose Stephen, a man full of faith and of the Holy Spirit, and Philip, **Prochorus, Nicanor, Timon, Parmenas** and **Nicolas,** a proselyte from Antioch. And these they brought before the apostles; and after praying, they laid their hands on them (Acts 6:5–6).

> Now there were at Antioch, in the church that was there, prophets and teachers: Barnabas, and Simeon who was called **Niger**, and **Lucius** of Cyrene, and Manaen who had been brought up with Herod the tetrarch, and Saul (Acts 13:1).

I wish I knew more about the rest of "the seven," as Luke calls them in Acts 21:8-9, and about those other names in Antioch overshadowed by Barnabas. Surely their service and efforts to teach were just as important in their respective places.

> … [Peter] went to the house of Mary, the mother of John who was also called Mark, where many were gathered together and were praying. When he knocked at the door of the gate, a servant-girl named **Rhoda** came to answer. When she recognized Peter's voice, because of her joy she did not open the gate, but ran in and announced that Peter was standing in front of the gate. They said to her, "You are out of your mind" (Acts 12:12–15).

Like Mary Magdalene, Joanna and Mary (Luke 24:1–11), Rhoda is another young woman appointed to bring good news to the disciples, whom they didn't initially believe. I wonder if the disciples own incidents of disbelief (Mark 16:11–16) helped make them more patient preachers when faced with others who refused to believe their eyewitness testimony, which is the basis of salvation (John 20:29; Acts 10:38–42)?

> After they had stopped speaking, **James** answered, saying, "Brethren listen to me" (Acts 15:13).

I would consider three James's to be *major* characters of the New Testament: the Apostle James the son of Zebedee who was martyred early (Acts 12:2); the Apostle James the son of Alphaeus; and James the brother of Jesus (Matthew 13:55; Galatians 1:19), who was considered "a pillar of the church" (Galatians 2:9), who spoke at the Jerusalem council, and who likely wrote the book of James. Especially for this last one, it's amazing to think how the resurrection (1 Corinthians 15:7) turned his skepticism (John 7:5) into faith.

> But the Jews, becoming jealous and taking along some wicked men from the market place, formed a mob and set the city in an uproar; and attacking the house of **Jason**, they were seeking to bring them out to the people ... and when they had received a pledge from Jason and the others, they released them (Acts 17:5–9).

I've always wanted to know if Jason's pledge violated his faith, or was it a perfectly neutral way to protect Paul?

> But some men joined [Paul] and believed, among whom also were **Dionysius** the Areopagite and a woman named **Damaris** and others with them (Acts 17:34).

Here in Athens, intelligence and faith and courage met, like it does today on college campuses. There may not be many like them among the scoffers, but their faith is often very strong.

**Crispus**, the leader of the synagogue, believed in the Lord with all his household, and many of the Corinthians when they heard were believing and being baptized (Acts 18:8).

Conversion accounts demand a series of their own, such as Simon the Sorcerer in Acts 8, the Ethiopian eunuch in Acts 8, Cornelius in Acts 10, the Philippian jailer in Acts 16. Really, they teach us more about the plan of salvation than about the contributions made by the individuals, and thus aren't really characters I wish to focus on here. However, I would like to mention Crispus. During Jesus' ministry, there were many rulers of the synagogue who believed in Jesus, but were not confessing Him for fear of losing power or being put out of the synagogue. This was not vanity—the synagogue was a Jewish person's whole life. Although there was so much at stake, John's ultimate conclusion is "they loved the approval of men rather than the approval of God" (John 12:43). Later, Paul mentions that Crispus was one of the few he personally baptized (1 Corinthians 1:14). In days soon to come, we will need some of that willingness to lose everything for Jesus.

And having sent into Macedonia two of those who ministered to him, Timothy and **Erastus**... (Acts 19:22).

Erastus is also mentioned in Romans 16:23 as "the city treasurer." An inscription has been found on a block of stone in Corinth bearing his name. It says, "Erastus, in return for his aedileship, paved it at his own expense." Christians in government are in a position of influence; they also are exposed to bitter persecution. It is heartening to see that Erastus is mentioned once again toward the end of Paul's life (2 Timothy 4:20).

...[Paul] decided to return through Macedonia. And he was accompanied by **Sopater** of Berea the son of Pyrrhus, and by **Aristarchus** and **Secundus** of the Thessalonians, and **Gaius** of Derbe, and Timothy, and Tychicus and **Trophimus** of Asia. But these had gone on ahead and were waiting for us at Troas (Acts 20:3-5).

Some of these men come up again. Paul calls Aristarchus a "fellow prisoner" in Colossians 4:10, and mentions him in Philemon 24. Paul recognizes Gaius as one whom he personally baptized (1 Corinthians 1:14) and as "host to me and the whole church" (Romans 16:23); perhaps he the same Gaius in Acts 19:29.

Trophimus is especially worthy of note. He must have been a frequent Gentile companion of Paul. In Acts 21:29, the Jews saw him hanging out with Paul in Jerusalem, and assumed Paul brought him into the Temple grounds where no Gentile is permitted to go, which instigated their mob violence. But more interesting to me, Trophimus experienced an illness many years later. Paul said flatly, "Trophimus I left sick at Miletus" (2 Timothy 4:20). Now, I often hear Pentecostals say that it is never God's will for a child of God to be sick, that all faithful people will be healed. Paul could perform miracles (Acts 19:12). Yet, God allowed him to remain sick. Obviously, the modern Pentecostal doctrine needs scrutiny.

> As we were staying there for some days, a prophet named **Agabus** came down from Judea. And coming to us, he took Paul's belt and bound his own feet and hands and said, "This is what the Holy Spirit says: 'In this way the Jews at Jerusalem will bind the man who owns this belt and deliver him into the hands of the Gentiles' (Acts 21:10–11).

It fascinates me that while Agabus spoke true prophecy, Paul did not interpret it as God's attempt to change his course. He continued toward Jerusalem ready to accept any fate.

> …we got ready and started on our way up to Jerusalem. Some of the disciples from Caesarea also came with us, taking us to **Mnason** of Cyprus, a disciple of long standing with whom we were to lodge (Acts 21:15–16).

New converts are exciting, but long-standing and trustworthy converts are important too!

But the **son of Paul's sister** heard of their ambush, and he came and entered the barracks and told Paul (Acts 23:16).

I wonder if Paul's nephew was a Christian, or just motivated by duty toward his own flesh and blood?

> ... Greet **Epaenetus**, my beloved, who is the first convert to Christ from Asia. Greet **Mary**, who has worked hard for you. Greet **Andronicus** and **Junias**, my kinsmen and my fellow prisoners, who are outstanding among the apostles, who also were in Christ before me. Greet **Ampliatus**, my beloved in the Lord. Greet **Urbanus**, our fellow worker in Christ, and **Stachys** my beloved. Greet **Apelles**, the approved in Christ. Greet those who are of the household of **Aristobulus**. Greet **Herodion** my kinsman. Greet those of the household of **Narcissus**, who are in the Lord. Greet **Tryphaena** and **Tryphosa**, workers in the Lord. Greet **Persis** the beloved, who has worked hard in the Lord. Greet **Rufus**, a choice man in the Lord, also **his mother** and mine. Greet **Asyncritus**, **Phlegon**, **Hermes**, **Patrobas**, **Hermas** and the brethren with them. Greet **Philologus** and **Julia**, **Nereus** and his sister, and **Olympas**, and all the saints who are with them. Greet one another with a holy kiss. All the churches of Christ greet you.
>
> Timothy my fellow worker greets you, and so do **Lucius** and **Jason** and **Sosipater**, my kinsmen. ... and **Quartus** the brother (Romans 16:5–16, 21, 23).

Notice the phrase, "in the Lord." When I count how many pagan Greco-Roman names are in this list—some drawn directly from the names of Greek deities—it's amazing to think how many Gentiles in Rome, brought up in and saturated with paganism, made the decision to repudiate the pantheon and all it represented, and instead make the good confession of Christ.

Also, I notice how many "worked hard" for the Lord and His body. Some, as a result of their bold faith, ended up with prison terms. Paul also highlights the contributions of women, who worked just as hard, and took just as many risks. I hesitate to make too much out of the meaning of the Greek roots of the names, but one pair stands out as humorous to me: Tryphaena means "dainty" and Tryphosa means "delicate," but these women were not afraid to get busy in the work of the Lord!

> Paul, called as an apostle of Jesus Christ by the will of God, and **Sosthenes** our brother, to the church of God which is at Corinth … (1 Corinthians 1:1–2).

In Acts 18:17, when Paul is being persecuted in Corinth, Sosthenes is the leader of the synagogue (apparently he replaced Crispus). He is beaten by the Jews in front of the judgment seat of Gallio. There must be quite a story of his conversion, and the Jews' increasing frustration!

> Now I urge you brethren (you know the household of **Stephanas**, that they were the first fruits of Achaia, and that they have devoted themselves for ministry to the saints), that you also be in subjection to such men and to everyone who helps in the work and labors. I rejoice over the coming of Stephanas and **Fortunatus** and **Achaicus**, because they have supplied what was lacking on your part. For they have refreshed my spirit and yours. Therefore acknowledge such men (1 Corinthians 16:15–18).

Paul mentions Stephanas at the start of the letter (1:16), that his household was one of the few he personally baptized. They went on to devote themselves to serving the brethren. Paul says that Christians should "acknowledge" such men and "be in subjection" to such men. I don't believe this is due to any authority, such as that wielded by elders (1 Timothy 5:17; Hebrews 13:17). It is simply a recognition that in devoting themselves to teaching and serving, their work is worth recognizing and encouraging (1 Thessalonians 5:11–13), and they deserve respectful consideration in what they say, since it comes from the perspective of those who study the Bible and demonstrate their care for the church.

But that you may know about my circumstances, how I am doing, **Tychicus**, the beloved brother and faithful minister in the Lord, will make everything known to you. I have sent him to you for this very purpose, so that you may know about us, and that he may comfort your hearts (Ephesians 6:21–22).

As to all my affairs, Tychicus, our beloved brother and faithful servant and fellow bond-servant in the Lord, will bring you information. For I have sent him to you for this very purpose, that you may know about our circumstances and that he may encourage your hearts; and with him Onesimus, our faithful and beloved brother, who is one of your number. They will inform you about the whole situation here (Colossians 4:7–9).

Tychicus is first mentioned with several others in Acts 20:3-5. Clearly, he was helpful to Paul in the work of evangelizing just as Timothy, Silas, and others.

I urge Euodia and I urge Syntyche to live in harmony in the Lord. Indeed, true companion, I ask you also to help these women who have shared my struggle in the cause of the gospel, together with **Clement** also and the rest of my fellow workers, whose names are in the book of life (Philippians 4:2-3).

The book of life—the only recognition that really matters!

Aristarchus, my fellow prisoner, sends you his greetings; and also Barnabas' cousin Mark (about whom you received instructions; if he comes to you, welcome him); and also Jesus who is called **Justus**; these are the only fellow workers for the kingdom of God who are from the circumcision, and they have proved to be an encouragement to me.

Greet the brethren who are in Laodicea and also **Nympha** and the church that is in her house (Colossians 4:10–11, 15).

What a work, to host the church, to open one's home to the brethren on a regular basis!

> Make every effort to come to me soon; for Demas, having loved this present world, has deserted me and gone to Thessalonica; **Crescens** has gone to Galatia, Titus to Dalmatia. Only Luke is with me. Pick up Mark and bring him with you, for he is useful to me for service. But Tychicus I have sent to Ephesus. When you come bring the cloak which I left at Troas with **Carpus**, and the books, especially the parchments.
>> Make every effort to come before winter. **Eubulus** greets you, also **Pudens** and **Linus** and **Claudia** and all the brethren (2 Timothy 4:9-13, 21).

> When I send **Artemas** or Tychicus to you, make every effort to come to me…. Diligently help **Zenas the lawyer** and Apollos on their way so that nothing is lacking them (Titus 3:12–13).

> …, to Philemon our beloved brother and fellow worker, and to **Apphia** our sister, and to Archippus our fellow soldier, and to the church in your house" (Philemon 1–2).

> Epaphras my fellow prisoner in Christ Jesus, greets you, as do Mark, **Aristarchus**, Demas, **Luke**, my fellow workers (Philemon 23–24).

Again, so many names whose contributions and journeys with Paul I wish I knew more about. Luke the physician could have his own entry, but I count him a major character requiring much study.

> The elder to the beloved **Gaius**, whom I love in truth (3 John 1).

Since Gaius was a very common name, this is probably a different individual than the one mentioned by Paul and Luke.

**Demetrius** has received a good testimony from everyone, and from the truth itself; and we add our testimony, and you know that our testimony is true (3 John 12).

Praise from fellow Christians who see your works is nice (Proverbs 27:2; 2 Thessalonians 1:4; 1 Thessalonians 3:6-7; Romans 16:19). But the greatest testimony of all comes from submission to God's truth!

In conclusion, may this unseen cloud of witnesses (Hebrews 12:1–2) spur us on toward the finish line!

## Questions for Thought

1. Pick one of the above names and describe what impressed you about his or her contribution to the Lord's work.

2. One more.

3. And one more.

# Conclusion

I HOPE YOU HAVE benefitted from these little portraits of often-overlooked Christians in Acts and the Epistles. There are so many wonderful stories of faith and victory hiding in those pages. Perhaps you've been inspired to hang on, to fight harder, to multiply good works in the kingdom. Each of these fellow workers was motivated by the greatness of God, by the love of Jesus, by the hope of Heaven.

While I look forward to learning their whole stories one day, meanwhile we too have our work to do upon the earth.

> Therefore, my beloved brethren, be steadfast, immovable, always abounding in the work of the Lord, knowing that your toil is not in vain in the Lord (1 Corinthians 15:58).

I read somewhere that the United States Air Force estimates it takes nineteen people to keep one pilot in the air. The pilot may perform spectacular maneuvers and drop precision bombs, but he couldn't do any of it without lots of help. There are mechanics to keep the planes flying, ordinance men to arm the bombs and load them onto the planes, air traffic controllers, mission planners and intelligence gatherers, radar operators, ship captains on aircraft carriers, satellite map readers, logistical officers, and many more. They don't get much recognition, but their jobs are crucial to the success of the Air Force. If the ordinance man improperly loaded the machine guns, the pilot would be in trouble when he squeezed the trigger in a dogfight. If the maintenance man failed to tune up the engines, the pilot would be in trouble when he accelerated off the deck. Why, even if the cook substituted decaf for regular coffee, the pilot might lose enough of his accustomed edge when he needed it most.

This study has helped me appreciate just how each and every person is vital to the work of the Lord, how each and every member is vital to the health of the body, how each and every laborer can rejoice in his part to play. "He who is faithful in a very little thing is faithful also in much" (Luke 16:10).

Let me bring this all to a close with a passage of Scripture:

> But, beloved, we are convinced of better things concerning you, and things that accompany salvation, though we are speaking in this way. For God is not unjust so as to forget your work and the love which you have shown toward His name, in having ministered and in still ministering to the saints. And we desire that each one of you show the same diligence so as to realize the full assurance of hope until the end, so that you will not be sluggish, but imitators of those who through faith and patience inherit the promises (Hebrews 6:9–12).

God has saved us. He has given us a job do to upon the earth, and inspirational examples of others who have gone before us. May we each demonstrate that we are inheritors of the promise by diligently contributing to the work of the Lord. The crown of life will make all our efforts worth it in the end.

Check out more of John Guzzetta's writing
from *Spiritbuilding Publishers*

*Strong marriages promote faithful children and active churches. In this book, John highlights many of the impressive couples revealed in the Bible. Whether you are married or are planning to marry, or know someone who is, this book provides a wonderful opportunity to explore God's will regarding the most important human relationship most of us will experience.*

Available at *spiritbuilding.com*

# Spiritbuilding
## PUBLISHERS

www.ingramcontent.com/pod-product-compliance
Lightning Source LLC
LaVergne TN
LVHW021342080426
835508LV00020B/2078